WE DON'T WANT
YOU,
UNCLE SAM

EXAMINING THE MILITARY
RECRUITING CRISIS
WITH GENERATION Z

Matthew Weiss

We Don't Want You, Uncle Sam: Examining the Military Recruiting Crisis with Generation Z
Published by Night Vision Publishing
Delray Beach, Florida

ISBN: 979-8-218-23666-3
POLITICAL SCIENCE / Public Policy / Military Policy

Publisher's Cataloging-in-Publication data

Names: Weiss, Matthew, author.
Title: We don't want you, Uncle Sam : examining the military recruiting crisis with Generation Z / Matthew Weiss.
Description: Delray Beach, Florida : Night Vision Publishing, [2023] | Includes bibliographical references.
Identifiers: ISBN: 979-8-218-23666-3
Subjects: LCSH: Military service, Voluntary--United States. | United States--Armed Forces--Recruiting, enlistment, etc.--Government policy. | United States--Armed Forces--Recruiting, enlistment, etc.--Case studies. | Generation Z--United States--Attitudes. | United States--Military policy. | BISAC: POLITICAL SCIENCE / Public Policy / Military Policy.
Classification: LCC: UB323 .W45 2023 | DDC: 355.2/230973--dc23
Interior design by Wolf Design and Marketing, wolfdesignandmarketing.com, copyright owned by Matthew Weiss.

NIGHT VISION
PUBLISHING

Dedicated to all those who have and will put on a uniform in defense of this great nation

Disclaimers

1. The views presented are solely those of the author and do not necessarily represent the views of the Department of Defense or its components.
2. No classified material was used in the production of this book. The Defense Office for Prepublication and Security Review has cleared this manuscript for release to the public.
3. No artificial intelligence was used to create the written content of this book. However, each internal image was generated with the assistance of AI.
4. This book was written with the intention of diagnosing and solving a real and serious issue facing our nation. No political party or agenda or group or mindset or ideology on either side will be pandered to in an attempt to fit any particular narrative. It's time we actually start putting in work and coming together to build a better future.

Please feel free to comment with your thoughts and ideas for solving the recruitment crisis on www.unclesambook.org

Contents

Generation Z has a meaning problem for what they call their "work." They need to have a calling that they strive deliberately towards. This calling has to be unique, larger than the individual, and impactful.

Solution: Establishing Military Meaning Mentorship (MMM) calls.

Competitive Zers want to signal that what they are doing is differentiated so they can rank themselves. The military should better display niche MOS communities, credentials, and clear billeting pipelines to attract competitive candidates.

Solution: The military must display niche MOS communities, credentials, and clear billeting pipelines to attract competitive candidates in small formalized group-chats (GTG = Good To Go Group).

Generation Z has a different relationship with religion than in the past. They often get their sense of morals and beliefs from a myriad of sources.

Solution: The military must tap into new, non-traditional outlets like influencers to reach Zoomers.

In order to help convince parents to support their children in joining the military, Veterans need to be inspired to transparently tell their past experiences.

Solution: All service members should be put in a college degree program to build toward their future so they want to help the institution once they are out of it.

Z has a tough balancing act between listening to elders' wisdom and having more knowledge than them. The recruiting job needs to work with this trend.

Solution: Recruiters should adopt a "keeping it real" approach, in concert with improving recruiter training and treatment though centralization, and applying a business-minded approach.

Gen Z has similar if not better physical health profiles than past generations, yet ridiculous medical standards prevent many from joining.

Solution: The entire health waiver process needs to be re-done, focusing only on if service members are physically able to do their future job or not.

PART II: WORKFORCE PARITY
Bringing Military Working Conditions In Line With Gen Z Expectations of The Modern Civilian Workplace

Everyone gets paid the same with no true reward structure. Pay in the military is incongruous in a generation that watches their peers gain followers through Youtube and Instagram. Better content, and better performance = more money.

Solution: The DoD should begin performance pay as bonuses for success, and money for food with a college-style meal plan to encourage healthiness and choice.

Gen Z wants to move faster, and there is a huge premium placed on time.

Solution: The option of shorter service contracts should exist.

The economic impact of recessions and boom cycles on joining the military make recruitment too cyclical.

Solution: Military recruitment needs to be detached from economic cycles by promoting side hustles and explaining pay in ways that are similar to other jobs.

INTRODUCTION:
The Current State of Military Recruiting

The current status of military recruiting in the United States is terrifyingly grim. Recruitment levels are at their lowest since the Vietnam era.[1] At a hearing on the issue in September of 2022, Senator Thom Tillis (R-NC) remarked, "There is no sunlight on the horizon. It's becoming clear the all-volunteer force that has served our country well over the last 50 years is at an inflection point." In the same hearing, Senator Kirsten Gillibrand (D-NY), pointed out, "By the end of 2022, the active U.S. military will be at its smallest size since the creation of the all-volunteer force."

While it's rare to see both political parties in such vehement agreement, the problem even caught the eye of former presidential candidate and billionaire tycoon Michael Bloomberg. In an article titled: "Military Recruitment Woes Endanger National Security,"[2] Bloomberg explained that, "To meet its overall goal of an active-duty force of 1.3 million, the military needs to bring in roughly 150,000 new recruits across its six service branches...By June, the Army had signed 22,000 troops, 60% below its annual target." When the 2022 fiscal year closed, the Army missed its year-end goal by roughly 15,000 Soldiers.

In summary, the numbers paint a bad picture, and 2023 is shaping up to be even worse. Even more concerning is the fact that the military recruits to its self-defined goals. Like any organization, these goals are just predictions of the manpower needed to operate given constrained resources. The projections often don't consider how many people we'd need in service to stave off some major existential war. In a modernized world with increasingly powerful adversaries and more countries with nuclear-capable threats, it's impossible to say how large the recruited force needs to be. Particularly when our strongest competitor, China, has more than 1 billion people than us. Even if we manage to barely hit our goal this year, the larger trendlines spell doom.

A better indicator than total recruit numbers is the desire generation Z has to serve. Regarding Z's propensity to enlist/commission, research by the RAND Corporation, reports that "propensity is generally low by historical standards, recently hovering around 13 percent for the general youth population aged 16-21."[3]

Perhaps most interesting in these discussions on military recruiting has been the reasons offered up as to why we're struggling to attract Gen Z. Deputy Assistant Secretary of Defense Stephanie Miller[4] states, "almost 44% of youth (ages 16 to 24) are ineligible for service," and "the department is examining our standards and entry programs, but alone, there is very little we can do to positively impact this issue."

The usual issues of drug abuse, educational level, obesity, and criminal records are often given as reasons why the qualification numbers sag.

However, the "Zoomer" generation, which Pew Research classifies as anyone born between 1997 and 2012,[5] has various unique reasons why they don't see the military as something they want to be a part of. From the fear of mental health disorders to a lack of interest, this new generation is turning sharply away from the armed services. Unfortunately, this comes at a time of rising international tension.

The overwhelming majority of new servicemembers fall between 17 and 30. Gen Z, whose average age is 17, is quickly becoming the only viable cohort of potential warfighters. A recent poll by the Ronald Reagan Institute showed less than one fifth of respondents aged 18-39 "extremely willing or very willing" to serve in the military while 26% were "not willing to serve at all."[6] If something doesn't happen to appeal to this age group, the country will soon jeopardize its national security.

I wrote this book to analyze the difficulties of recruiting Zoomers and propose a variety of interventions aimed at getting my generation to serve in uniform. I realized that no D.C. politician or big brass general seems to have the correct solutions to this problem. So, I reasoned that perhaps one young and lost Gen-Z Lieutenant, describing his own modern life thoughts, may shed light on what we're searching for.

This book has three main audiences. The largest audience members are those concerned with the state of our military and its vital role in national defense. The more targeted audience members are those with the power to enact change on the issue of recruiting. This includes Congress, generals/admirals, the press, engaged public voters, and DoD civilians. A significant number of Americans are well aware of the growing recruitment issues that endanger our military. Many reports, congressional hearings, and newspaper articles have been written in an attempt to figure this out. A cornerstone argument I make here is that only older decision-makers, who are far too detached from the root problems, are tasked with solving it. While I don't have anywhere near the experience and wisdom of these leaders, I am a member of the very generation that they are trying to recruit. This problem is one that requires deep knowledge that is distributed only at the "tactical" level. Kat Cole, an amazing business executive who spoke to me in college, explained that in organizations, most problems are solved by those closest to them. Admirals in the Pentagon and representatives in Congress aren't going to understand the generational feelings of Americans in their late teens and early twenties. Only the young Americans who actually make up generation Z can truly understand this.

Finally, this was written for the current Gen Zers in service and those about to be. Hopefully I can do my small part to better our military, which each of you have given so much to. It is our job to get our ideas out there and impact where we work, even if we don't exactly know how best to say what we're trying to articulate. I ask all of you to take some moments of reflection and reaffirm your principles and determine what type of leaders you want to be and why you joined the armed forces. Ours is one of the few jobs where doing so may literally and directly save lives. We have a duty to improve the institution we're a part of, and the one we'll lead one day.

The book is broken down into four distinct parts:

I. **Recruiting Fundamentals** = Analyzing the basics of Gen Z recruitment

II. **Workforce Parity** = Bringing military working conditions in line with Gen Z expectations of the modern civilian workplace

III. **Sociocultural Influences** = Viewing aspects of larger society that impact Gen Z military recruitment

IV. **Scope of Service** = Promoting ways in which the military can give back to society

Within each part exist detailed chapters explaining a particular problem and proposing a possible solution. My goal is to shed light on various American practices that may be hurting modern day military recruitment from the perspective of a new servicemember. Ideally I can arm these decision-makers with a deeper understanding of what is going on, while also suggesting some solutions they can implement. While I don't expect readers to agree with each issue and suggestion, I believe that each one prompts deep thought and debate. My hope is that the developed compendium will explain how we must rebuild the value proposition of military service by demonstrating the benefits of the world's greatest physical social network.

The chapters include a mix of statistics, literature analysis, and sometimes small vignettes that demonstrates a key life lesson I've had. These small moments make up my personal story, and in the spirit of my grandfather, who explained that "stories are what makes the world go around," I will do my best to share them in a way that benefits my readers. My life journey that saw myself, an unlikely candidate to put on the uniform, as a Marine Intelligence Officer, is interwoven throughout. I am fully aware of the many biases and blind spots that come with my unique life experience. If you ask one thousand people why they joined the military you may very well get one thousand different responses. The stories are used to tie a common thread and personal touch to a multilayered, macro-level issue. At times we forget that every young American who signs up to take that oath of office into America's military is their own unique individual with their own way of thinking. The writing has allowed me to nostalgically recall various events over my Gen-Z existence and helped frame my beliefs on where I think the military should be going. To begin I want to give a very basic overview of myself and why I felt qualified to opine on this topic.

I was born a day after tax day in New York City as the first child to my very supportive parents. At age two we moved to the suburban town of Tenafly, New Jersey where I attended the Tenafly Public School system from kindergarten through 12th grade. I am the older brother to three younger siblings whom I try to be a role model for everyday. I had four very loving grandparents and was blessed to be able to travel the world with my family on exotic vacations. I attended The Wharton School at the University of Pennsylvania in Philadelphia for both my undergraduate degree in Finance and Management and my Masters in Business Administration with a concentration in Information Systems. While in college I was the co-chair of the Admissions Dean's Advisory Board, where I got an excellent viewpoint of how one of the world's most selective Universities attracts talent. I worked at various summer internships in financial companies and got my first full-time job doing mergers and acquisitions at a Defense Technology Startup that is now a Silicon-Valley multi-billion-dollar unicorn. That incredible success story has succeeded in attracting world class talent from generation Z and faces the opposite problem of military recruitment: they have too many applicants. I am currently a Lieutenant in the United States Marine Corps. As a Military Intelligence Officer, I specialize in Signals Intelligence/Electronic Warfare.

I fundamentally believe that my upbringing, education at Wharton, and experiences in the entry-level of the tech/finance world have provided me with unique mental frameworks from which to help answer this question about recruitment. The world's oldest business school taught me to use financial thinking to make decisions, one of the country's fastest growing companies showed me recruiting gone right, and the USMC intelligence mindset has taught me to properly prioritize analysis. Throughout the course of the book I will incorporate thoughts from each of these institutions. Above all I am a patriot, looking to do my part in uniting our great Country. On a personal level, when I didn't think I'd make it through boot camp (OCS) and actually commission, my meanest and toughest drill instructor challenged me to leave the organization better than when I found it. I promised I would...this is my attempt to fulfill that promise.

Analyzing the Basics of Gen Z Recruitment

The year was 1998. As the very first members of our new generation took their initial breaths of life, the world was about to undergo a seismic economic shift. This change saw a post-industrial economy transform into a technological one. Everything was moving online and the earth's information needed to be sorted. Google was founded, and humanity's thoughts were forever organized into easily accessible pages. The babies born with me became the first to have all their questions answered with the click of a button.

Growing up, my family encouraged me to ask adults many questions. Five years later, during my grandfather's birthday, I tried querying his fellow seventy-year-olds. I didn't know much about life, but with all the childhood innocence I could muster, I led off with, "what did you do for a living?" The retiree attendees cracked up. They found it hilarious that this chubby, bowl-haircut child was asking them about their former professions. "I'm a lawyer, I deal with something called the law, but really it means I read a lot every day." "I'm a doctor; I work to help heal people's bodies when they get sick." "I'm a businessman; I sell things to make money." I didn't realize it then, but I was conducting an experiment that struck at the core of American identity.

The six chapters that comprise part one lay out some fundamental characteristics related to this new generation and our views on the world. In order to solve the recruiting crisis, we have to first grasp just how different Z is compared to past age cohorts. When it comes to our views around what is meaningful and what we desire from our work, it's essential that the recruiting establishment change its entire mindset to understand who we are. I argue that our views look very different than past generations', like my grandfather's, which served in the major wars of the 20th century because of the time period and technological change we've been impacted by. Unlike millennials, we're actually a competitive generation who needs to be reached in more modern ways. I analyze the ways that Z's nature makes us harder to recruit under our current system, and explore some current health standards that hold that system back. The section ends with discussions on some of those external influencers such as our parents, millennial Veterans, and modern recruiters themselves.

CHAPTER 1:
Understanding the Meaning Behind Work

T he way Americans respond to the question of what they do for a living is very revealing of how they view their work. One seminal organizational behavior study on work categorizes people into three groups: those that view what they do as a job, a career, or a calling.[7] The job group is those who work to live and support their lifestyles and families. A career mindset is a middle group that focuses on advancement, achievement, and growth. Finally, those who consider what they do a calling believe that their work is a crucial part of their identity. For this final group, work is their life and vice versa. Generation Z's relationship with work mainly falls into this third and final category.

With the onset of the COVID lockdowns and remote tasking, scores of employees quit their jobs and began questioning their relationship with work. Undoubtedly, these questions reached the family dinner table with developing Gen Zers eagerly listening. Under the surface emerged a new trend that Harvard Professor Ranjay Gulati calls "the great rethink.[8]" As Gen Z's parents began reflecting and rethinking their work, the door swung open for the newest working generation to do the same, even before many had formally entered the labor force. When discussing amongst each other and within their own heads, many Zers discovered they had a meaning problem for what they call their "work." Meaning trumps most other factors in determining how a Zer chooses a job. This generation feels it needs to have a calling that they work deliberately towards. This calling has to be unique, more significant than the individual, and impactful.

Generation Z wants their calling to be unique to them. Stanford Researcher Roberta Katz analyzed millions of snippets of Gen Z online speech in a project called iGen Corpus. One of her main discoveries is that Gen Z emphasizes finding unique identities.[9] Verbiage is a crucial consideration here in defining a unique meaning. If someone is a doctor, while that is admirable and respectable in society, they are just one of the roughly one million doctors in the U.S.[10] One level above that is the neurosurgeon, an extremely rare and niche doctor, but still one of thousands. Neither of those two descriptions is particularly unique.

A calling, however, is usually a sentence, a string of words put together in a fundamentally differentiated way. Just like a mission statement in a military order, a calling usually has a "why" attached to it. In the military, this why comes in the format "in order to" and comprises the commander's intent, a concept nearly all those in the armed forces understand. It is the purpose behind the order, the reason "why" for doing something. Generation Z, often without explicitly realizing it, actually sees their callings in a similar way. An example would be, "I want to go into healthcare to protect the elderly from disease because my grandmother suffered tremendously from COVID."

The generation cares less about the rigid doctor title and more about the destination, "I want to go into healthcare." The reasoning behind the meaning "because my grandmother suffered tremendously from COVID" makes the calling uniquely different. Scores of Zers may want to go into healthcare, much fewer because their grandmother got COVID. On the flip side, potentially thousands of Zers had grandmothers with COVID, but not all of them want to go into healthcare, particularly for the reason to "protect the elderly from disease." Gen Z is more likely to answer the question with a verb rather than a noun. I counsel, I teach, I save lives are more appealing than I am a counselor, I am a teacher, or I am a nurse. While many in the generation are still growing up and figuring out their exact calling sentence, the traits of these new workers lead them to want to make that sentence unique to their own lives. Notably, they want to be able to say or post something to the larger society that scores them social standing. With millions of online accounts, another stereotypical doctor or lawyer isn't giving anyone extra points. However, the person who studied law in order to debate human rights at the international court is someone whom their Z peers will quickly laud for being different.

It's essential to recognize the significant time period that generation Z has developed in. From this lens, their desire to have meaningful work that is larger than themselves seems logical. This generation is the first that was either not yet born or was too young to remember 9/11. Z came of processing age and learned about it as part of history class or an early discussion with a parent. That paradigm-shifting military event that defined the millennial generation's Global War on Terror does not hold the same effect on generation Z. Instead, Z had their childhoods book-ended with the Great Financial Crises and the COVID-19 pandemic. These large-scale, global events impacted nearly everyone in the world and caused great domestic strife. Both events subsequently shaped a deep desire to do work that reaches broad audiences. The traditional barriers of the globe are now eliminated with a generation that has been used to getting Wi-Fi and an iPhone at nearly the same time they grew out of diapers. This mass communication combined with technology makes Gen-Z think of their work as globally reaching. The Zoomer genera-tion is one of "influencers," who can legitimately reach an audience of millions in seconds. Z expects their work to do much the same. They care less about how their work betters themselves or helps them grow on the small or local level, and much more about how their work is larger than any one individual. The creation of a viral video trend is now seen as the epitome of child fame. This stirs a desire in Z for work that can spread to similar viral lengths.

To Z, impactful work yields results that can be immediately observed. In prior times, long-term projects seemed noble, and society rewarded non-myopic thinking. Now, the entire world moves faster and expects quicker results. If someone wants to order a taxi, Uber has one within 10 minutes. If someone wants to buy an item, Amazon will deliver it within two days. This "instant" economy makes the world seem like it is spinning faster. Parents today, members of generation X, had time to adapt to these speed changes. Generation Z was born right into them and has known nothing else in life. A famous computer adage related to this called Moore's law says, "speed and capability of computers can be expected to double every two years."[11] While Gen Zers themselves are not computers, their brains have been so impacted by them that it would be folly not to examine if a similar human phenomenon was occurring.

Now, evolution and hereditary brain change isn't happening as rapidly as two years. However, the passage of time within the lens of technology does actually seem to be moving this rapidly. Interestingly, a study[12] done during COVID captured this phenomenon. Time expansion is that strange feeling many experienced but couldn't describe in lockdown where time either sped up or slowed down at abnormal rates. The study showed that with age, those participants that were younger, felt the slowdown of time the most. The corollary to Moore's law concerning the fast and immediate pace of the modern world can be dubbed the "time law." The time law plays with our perception of time, where, with new apps and technologies coming out every day, our world seems to be moving ever-faster. Relating this to Gen Z's need for immediately impactful work, Zers aren't inclined to wait around to see results that may take ten years to mature. Generation Z wants their callings to produce immediate changes in the world around them. They'd rather see a minor change now than a much more significant change over a much larger period of time. Just like in finance, with how the time value of money is discounted at some rate as years go by, perceived work impact is reduced as days linger. Z will sacrifice quality or depth for immediacy, which is possibly the value-maximizing strategy in their hypersonic world.

The challenge for the modern military is how to capitalize on Gen Z's desire to have a calling, not just a job. Unfortunately, an increasing gap is opening between military service and the perception of a calling. Recruiters are struggling to create innovative marketing to explain what used to be obvious. Service used to be one of the highest-extolled virtues; arguably, nothing was more meaningful. In WWII everyone served and if you didn't you were stigmatized. Today, it's increasingly difficult to convince Zoomers that giving up rights and privileges to take on duties and responsibilities in uniform is the right path. Are Z's new callings so out of touch with the traditional military? Is there an unmendable gap trying to be crossed by some alone and unafraid recruiter who just started the job? No, but the only people to enlighten future Z recruits on how the military can help achieve their callings, are those Zers currently in the military. Only fellow Gen-Zers actually understand this generation's deep quest for a calling. That strange feeling of being in a virtual sea of millions, wanting to be noticed for doing something different, yet still fitting in at the same time.

This yearning is subconscious, created by a myriad of societal factors that have shaped young people. Therefore, the marketing messaging put forth by the Armed Forces also has to target the subconscious via deep, similar-aged conversations rather than billboard messaging. Dr. Tim Elmore, the writer of "Generation Z Unfiltered,"[13] explains that more kids today have an increasingly external locus of control. They look to the outside world for the answers to why things are happening to them. This is a very prohibitive mindset with actual negative results attached to it.[14] Essentially those with an external locus think the outside world controls their destiny, and that they are almost powerless to change their fate. No Zer says outright, "I feel as though there is an external locus of control over my life." Instead, the thinking develops on a much deeper level due to the struggles currently enveloping society. One small example of this is McKinsey's American Opportunity Survey, which shows generation Z's financial trepidation. Nearly 23% of the ~25,000 respondents queried say they don't expect ever to retire. Only 41% ever hope to own a home[15].

While this may be youthful naivete, the genuine dread is often palpable. The delivered military messaging has to focus on putting that control back into the hands of Zers. Explaining that the military itself can be a way to make sense of this rapidly changing world is a start. The military must present itself as a way to carve a calling that is unique to each recruit, is more significant than that person, and is one where real impacts will be observed during their time in service. While all of that sounds like nice words for an overpaid consultant to put on a PowerPoint slide, there needs to be real, pragmatic action that those at the lower ranks in the military can take to re-link service and calling.

For me, this happened during the single most important lesson I ever had in business school. In fact, if I could do only one exercise from my five years at Wharton again it would be this one. We were tasked with reading the six minute article "How Will You Measure Your Life?" by the legendary Clayton Christensen[16] (anyone reading this book should immediately read it, as it will benefit your existence more than anything else you do this year). Our professor then explained that if businesses have mission statements, it would be pretty logical if all of us sat down once and wrote a personal meaning statement for life. Such a quick task took hours of thinking, but it forced us to put into writing what we were doing on earth. It helped us develop the unique, significant, and timely reason we woke up for the work we were planning to do everyday. The only way an exercise so simple yet impactful as this can reach new recruits and enable them to see military service as a calling will be through determined Z mentorship.

The military meaning mentorship or triple M initiative would be a mandatory DoD program for current Gen Z servicemembers. It would require those with at least six months in uniform to provide ten hours per year to have phone conversations with possible new joiners. Recruiters could select from a branch/job/geography-specific list. They could then connect them with one potential recruit to be matched for a one-hour, Z-Z, heart-heart, meaning discussion. In it, the servicemember and new Z recruit craft calling statements and answer questions to help explain how the military delivers the unique impact that the recruit is desiring.

This program would codify what is already unofficially occurring. Many Z service members currently have mentorship calls with hometown friends about the military, but it's done in a one-off and disaggregated way. The program would formalize the requirement and help recruiters better find similarity-matched servicemembers to talk to. Studies show that time spent giving back to an organization's future while engaging in mentoring, yields positive mental results and better work outcomes for the mentor too.[17] If colleges have campus tours where current students are the guides rather than admissions officers, recruits should be able to speak to current service members (their future selves) rather than just recruiters. This new program would take that meaningful event I experienced from behind the doors of academia and democratize it to each uniformed service member. It would be such a simple, quick, and effective way of utilizing the young manpower of the military to give back and direct Americans into planning a better path for their lives.

Now, like with any program, there will be outliers and some certain failures. If more than 180,000 service members were now ordered to have one phone call a year, there will likely be thousands of mismatched conversations and ineffective results. However, Zers are eager to share their ideas on their mission with other people also on a mission. An example of this would be after following a prompted question, a new recruit saying, "I want to join the military to learn how to lead others so that I can one day be the head of my household while also caring for my aging parents." The Zer in uniform could explain, "I prevent cyberattacks from hurting our nation because a cyberhacker impacted my personal savings." There are millions of calling statements the pairs will inevitably discuss, but the main point is that discussing meaning with a Zer creates a mentorship network where both parties benefit and improve their understanding of their military calling.

For Gen Z, what is meaningful also needs to be reinforced by what is measurable. Competition is a key way Zers measure and differentiate themselves, which is explored in chapter 2.

CHAPTER 2:
Differentiating Through Competition

The ~70 million kids who have grown up hunting for likes, retweets, and shares are now becoming young adults who want to compete in the working world. Z has nurtured a mindset that allows them to do activities and make proclamations that rank them in society. David and Jonah Stillman,[18] the authors of "Gen Z at work," explain that Gen Z believes there are winners and losers in the world. In high school, the likes one receives on a Facebook picture or the following-follower ratio one has on Instagram signifies social status. Z now realizes that these metaphysical bits and bytes, which confer "points" in youth, can also be obtained in adulthood. This social competition leads to a strong desire for signaling amongst Zoomers. Tons of research literature[19] is focused on analyzing social hierarchies. For all their lamentable aspects, they fulfill innate human needs for resource allocation and understanding in a way that motivates.

History has long recognized social capital and status. However, today's modern digital teenager has a more transparent, more instant, and more public accounting system to do so. Three converging trends are heavily influencing today's hierarchies. Firstly, niche communities are making social rankings more focused. Second, this ranking system is often tabulated by the visual progress one can project and display. Third, Zers want to know the clearly defined paths to climbing in these hierarchies; the so-called rules for winning. Overall, this digital game Zers are used to playing presents an opportunity for the military to capitalize on. The military should better display niche MOS communities, credentials, and clear billeting pipelines to attract competitive candidates.

Zoomers need to find their niche communities to compete in. Smaller niches help break down this giant, confusing, and ever-expanding world. The United States Department of Defense is the largest employer in the country if you also count the non-uniformed civilian employees. The service branches are giant and not monolithic. In the Army (the largest branch) and the Marine Corps, troops are assigned military occupational specialties (MOS) to designate their job codes. For enlisted Soldiers, the Army alone has nearly 190 different MOS ranging from infantryman to plumber. Each of these career fields has different levels of density, meaning the manpower in each is not distributed evenly. By nature of the different tasks that make up MOS, often unique communities with different hierarchies form. In any given operational unit, there will likely be a healthy mix of many MOS. However, those with the same MOS often end up working together. Even more significant is that MOS train together at various military school houses across the country. After boot camp and a short amount of basic service-wide training, new joins immediately ship off to their MOS- producing courses, where they begin establishing these niche communities. It is a crucial time period because it often occurs within the first year of entering the military.

A prospective Gen Zer with a propensity to compete and join the military, may quickly be overwhelmed by the large entry classes they'll be placed in. Imagine saying to a person who went to a high school with 100 people that in a few months if they sign on the dotted line they'll be expected to perform with thousands of new recruits. That concept naturally evokes fear and negates any hopes of thriving in a competition. Those entry-level numbers are literally too big for the teenage brain to make sense of. In the popular press, there is the notion that a human can only successfully maintain social connections with around 150 people.[20] There is no question that Zers can only participate in accurately judged hierarchies with some reasonable limit on the number of people involved. The stress this new and large hierarchy group will elicit ends up negating the same benefits of competition in the first place. One *Harvard Business Review* article notes that while competition often motivates people and encourages more effort to achieve results, the competitions need to elicit excitement rather than anxiety.

I remember my own excitement at my first elementary-school soccer tryouts. I knew that even if I wasn't good enough to make the A-team, I'd have a spot on the B-team, so all my anxiety was gone. We lost most of our games, but at the end of the season, I asked my Mom if she could buy me a medal. Now, based on the popular press about newer generations, most would assume that my mother went to the nearest convenience store and got me the shiniest participation trophy she could find. Absolutely not. Her stern response was, "You didn't win anything; you only get a medal if you win." Unlike their millennial counterparts, Z does not come from the "everyone gets a trophy" generation. We are fiercely competitive and will outcompete our peers with a "whatever it takes" attitude to get what [we] want."[21] Z doesn't like medals for showing up. We want to prove we're more worthy than our peers and display medals for superior achievement. This requires competitions to be framed correctly and scoped appropriately[22]. The task for recruiters here is to break down the massive size of the military into something smaller that recruits can understand. Comprehending large data in large groups is not our strength. After all, our generation is used to consuming content in tiny, 5-second videos and memes.

That "something smaller" is the niche MOS communities. These can bring out a more manageable type of competition. If that same recruit knew the density and population of their future MOS, and if they were adequately informed that their follow-on schoolhouse would likely have a much smaller class size, they would feel differentiated and better prepared to "flex" on the competition. As Z competes in these hierarchies that they're so used to measuring, they want to feel that their hierarchy is apart from the rest, that it is distinct, separate, and manageable. It wasn't just the Bin Laden raid that made special operations sexy in the minds of American youth. The words "special operations" denote a sense of superiority, distinction, and being better than the rest. This is a natural draw for a generation that doesn't want to sit around climbing a massively large corporate ladder. Instead, we'd rather use some new technology to pole vault up a mini-stool. By better understanding the future niche communities they may be a part of, a recruit will have a higher competitive drive and knowledge of how they can handle the social hierarchy they are hoping to compete in.

Generation Z wants to display its credentials to its select communities. The world is placing a growing premium on ostentatious displays.

While colorful fireworks have been around for centuries and the bright lights of Times Square have attracted tourists for decades, the modern Zer looks at more content through their eyes by the time they reach age 18 than any of their ancestors combined. Z's parents may have played classical board games like chess and listened to rock music on a record player, but Z grew up racing cars on Xbox live and watching music videos to match the latest techno D.J. remix. Zoomers are on pixel overload, making the way they communicate with each other very visual. There is more scientific research on vision than any other sensory modality because of how America has socially and culturally aligned its society.[23] We've designed a world in which what we see is what we perceive. Our desires strongly shape the way we process the visual data our eyes collect[24]. Z isn't looking for job titles but rather badges, tags, and public credentials. There is a major attempt to display the unique skills that individual is bringing to their group. Badging plays into Z's deep-seated desire to show others what they know and what they can do. The modern-day corollary of posting a good report card on a fridge with a magnet is having a lengthy list of badges to show off on LinkedIn.

The military already does its own form of badging with hard-earned medals and ribbons. The defense community's pride in donning its dress uniforms has always communicated an organization keen on displaying achievement. Most of those awards signify incredible victories earned through years of hard work. Some patches and devices feature skills-specific milestones like parachute jumps, flying wings, and dive bubbles. However, most of these are physical, worn on the uniform every day, or reserved just for formal events. In the digital realm, badging has grown much faster in the private sector, with the military playing catch-up. While the military formerly developed some of the best management practices that American corporations have long benefitted from, the pendulum has now reversed. It's time for modern businesses to teach the military new 21st-century ideas and methods. Senior program executive at IBM David Leaser writes, "Digital badges have provided value in every area we measure, including identifying and acquiring verified talent."[25] Currently, though, usage of badging is non-existent in the recruiting realm. The #hashtag generation ascribes real meaning to those tags they seemingly pin on every post. Tagging, arguably the digital version of graffiti, is an act of visual expression, and it denotes acquired skills and beliefs that help Zers compete.

Zoomers crave certainty in their planning, something direct billeting pathways can offer. This generation naturally likes code, if not for the understanding of its beautiful complexity than for the gratefulness for all it has enabled. The incredible thing about code is that it lays out a clear-cut direction for a computer processor to execute. While it's often extolled that Zers abhor the proven and extoll the non-traditional, in reality, clear-cut, tried-and-true pathways are something many Zers believe in. The rise of "how to" videos are a direct testament to this. Zers are hunting for a guidebook to follow in a world of uncertainty. Uncertainty[26] causes aversion in the amygdala and insula parts of our brains. FMRI imaging showed that when presented with uncertain stimuli, human participants consistently overestimated the frequency with which aversive images would follow. People are literally hard-wired to reduce situations that cause stress or unease, and uncertainty is precisely one of those situations.

A laid-out journey that highlights what to expect will appeal more to a Zer than even one with higher potential rewards but many more unknowns. The military's challenge here is to successfully explain career progression and accurately forecast training pathways while remaining flexible enough to respond to crises and changing world threats. One niche part of military recruiting is the direct commissioning/direct entry programs. These unique pipelines are usually for cyber specialists, Judge Advocate Generals (lawyers), band members, Navy Seals, and other highly specialized fields. The premise with direct commissioning is that these jobs are so unique and require such specialized skills, that when signing your contract you are guaranteed a particular route through your military career. The traditional uncertainty of the MOS process is removed from this because direct commissions usually have only one or two training schools at well-established and non-changing locations. Direct commissioning paths are not going to replace traditional MOS placement. That said, the idea of taking a recruit and explaining the entire pipeline from the start of training toward a final billet, where advancement is visible and understood, adds a critical level of certainty.

One way for prospective new recruits to see their own unique communities, display their skills, and understand their possible career paths is to create tailored group chats early on in the recruiting process. American colleges are consistently ranked top in the world, and with around one million international students, more foreigners choose to go to school here than in any other nation.[27] It would benefit the military recruiting apparatus to adopt some techniques these institutions use to attract talent. Colleges fight fiercely to hit enrollment and matriculation numbers. One of their techniques is when they invite admitted students into small groups and Facebook pages before the school year to meet other interested students. These pre-orientation chats are informal, sometimes culminating with zoom discussions with peers. The chats help foster interpersonal friendships and allow future students to get a "feel" for who their future classmates might be if they choose that school. The military should do the same with small, formalized group chats called "Good To Go Groups." Many of these small text chats often already happen informally between recruiters and potential joiners. The Good to Go Groups would instead be a more deliberate approach where recruits can connect with each other before deciding to join.

The small groups should be based on prospective MOS preferences/ communities. The recruiters who establish the group can send an introductory text template explaining some possible topics for chatting and breaking the ice with initial introductions. Those initial intros can be essentially badging opportunities, "John is from Texas. He's studying SQL after school and plays varsity basketball." The recruiter should then leave the chat and allow the ~5 prospects to form connections themselves. To borrow Jeff Bezos's two-pizza rule at Amazon,[28] the ideal group number of 5-8 people best facilitates meaningful connections without getting too large. These groups should specifically be people who don't live near each other or have the same recruiter, but instead be based on related interests in MOS. For example, if a group of new recruits interested in Infantry could be introduced, they might be able to share workouts and meal prep ideas together. Similarly a group of intel specialists could explain how they're thinking about their current cyber and technical skills.

After the initial setup, the workload falls away, and the flywheel effect of having young American Zers chat over text with other Zers takes place. These groups would help bring out healthy competition as they research and navigate the pipelines they'd be going through if they joined. It also enables each recruit to pool information since they'd be from different recruiters, so they can work to build each other's knowledge. Understanding what their future niche communities would look like, and explaining what they're already doing in high school to each other, would foster a healthy amount of competition. "I found this; you guys should check out what training we go through," and "my recruiter just told me about this new program; check it out," are perfect examples of beneficial conversations in one of these groups. In the end, the networks the groups created would increase conversion by helping to break away from the current norm - of falling out of touch with the recruiting process due to lack of continuity. Prospective recruits in the contemplation stages would essentially be working to convince each other to join.

Shrinking the imposing size of the military down into more manageable groups for recruits will help reduce uncertainty and foster community. Today, current communities of Zers are being influenced by forces very different from those seen in the past. The next chapter explores some of those influences and explains how the military can work with them.

CHAPTER 3:

Reaching a Changing Congregation

Regardless of the various views on religion, one undeniable fact is that Generation Z is poised to be the least religious generation in the history of America. As a practicing Jew who had a Bar Mitzvah and attempts to observe the Sabbath every week, I've watched my faith leaders decry the "great secularization" of today's youth. Many of my Christian, Hindu, and Muslim peers have witnessed a similar trend. Without exploring the causes of this, the military should recognize and adapt accordingly.

Religion and the United States military have long been linked together. Our citizens were religious, so naturally, the military was, too. The close connection between beliefs in God and the afterlife to the permanent and often deadly nature of warfare may also explain the intense relationship. War is the most horrible and dangerous act humans engage in. With our strong survival instincts and terror of dying,[29] religion often helps bring meaning to the actions armies are forced to commit. The military has long fought to bring the religious freedoms experienced here in the United States to nations we've fought for and against. It has also gone to great lengths to support servicemembers' religious practices, sometimes even in dangerous combat situations. The military officially recognizes over 220 religions[30] (including atheism) and has a large and diverse chaplain corps of ~2,800 faith leaders. Sadly, even the Chaplain corps is now facing recruitment issues.

A leading poll shows an estimated 48% of generation Z has no religious affiliation[31]. Another Pew poll shows that Christianity, which has been and will continue to be the largest religion in the United States, will have its worshippers make up less than 47% of the entire population by 2070.[32] That isn't an affront against the church, which has unified and nurtured our nation for hundreds of years. It's simply an accurate and truthful depiction of current reality. With religion among American youth down, the military must tap into new, non-traditional outlets from which Z gets its sense of morals and beliefs.

It's important to analyze religion's role in military recruitment so far. It has been proven that highly religious young men without a college degree are more likely to enlist in the military than those who identify as not religious.[33] The American church establishment has greatly supported military recruitment efforts throughout history. There is no question that the centralized organization provided by the institution of churches has boosted accession by spreading a message of service.

Firstly, churches have been great gathering places upholding the community and providing recruiters with the ability to influence many potential recruits all at once. Surveys show that religious Americans participate in community social events 14% more when compared to non-religious Americans[34]. Secondly, the messages spread by religious groups about giving back to the country and serving others have undoubtedly fostered an increase in the mindset of making sacrifices and giving back. Lastly, the structure of the Christian church has enabled new generations to be brought up with a sense of learning, values, and beliefs passed down from the older generations and the Bible. All of this is to say that to reach the young Americans who remain religious and attend religious services, recruiters should and will continue to rely partially on faith and faith-based organizations to achieve numbers.

However, to impact this new half of non-religious youth, the recruiting establishment must bring something different to the altar. Much has been written about influencers and how they use information to shape particular narratives and share their viewpoints. Gen Z follows influencers more than anyone, and entire marketing companies have been created to make money on this trend. More interesting than the products and ideas these influencers are pedaling are the underlying reasons Z brains are flocking to them for advice and guidance. One McKinsey analysis draws a critical distinction between the new generation Z and the older millennials finding, "For example, while both age groups look to social media, they do so differently: millennials are more apt to consult the hive mind—the online collective—whereas Gen Zers seek out those they believe are in the know."[35] For some, instead of listening to pastors and preachers for life advice, social media influencers are legitimately the new guides for Z. One Deputy Assistant Secretary of Defense acknowledges, "What we really want to be able to do here is to be able to provide more personalized and tailored content. What we are really right now is a blunt force instrument, and we want to be more strategic. We want to be able to kind of package our messaging so that it can resonate with greatest effect to a generation where we count seconds in terms of being able to capture their attention."[36] A sniper-rifle-tailored approach rather than a wide shotgun blast is needed. After all, access to an influencer can happen 24/7 with finger movements on an iPhone, while a bible is often only read at the pew on Sundays. In terms of sheer attention minutes, Z spends more time listening to their favorite online disciples than almost anyone else (including their parents). Even those Zers that are religious have prolific online faith influencers to tap into.

In summary, Z likes listening to advocates they relate to and seek out, rather than those forced upon them due to affiliation. The overarching point is that niche, online personas are now fulfilling a new role in society that previously only religion had dominion over. This role, while sometimes only providing fashion trends and products, also often educates the next generation about morals and values, and provides lifestyle blueprints. Z is much more likely to consider themselves spiritual rather than religious. Life guidance to Zoomers is more like a salad bar, mixing a little bit of Jesus, Buddha, Ronaldo, McConaughey, Shelton, and Kardashian. Together, their opinions get thrown into a big bowl of guidelines for Zers to make decisions, and act according to what they believe in.

Currently, the Army identifies three gaps when trying to persuade Z to join: identity, knowledge, and trust. The identity gap stems from Zers' inability to picture themselves in the military. The knowledge gap is when the brand and reality of what the military has to offer is not reaching Zoomers. Finally, the trust gap has emerged with this generation not believing in one of America's historically most trusted institutions.

Enticed correctly, approved social media influencers can be the solution needed to fill these gaps. Zers trust them, try to emulate them and their lifestyles, and are very familiar with their carefully cultivated brands. Zers, unlike their parents, understand how modern media marketing works. They grasp the fundamental principles of search engine optimization and similar video suggestions. It's not a surprise to Z when after talking with their Aunt about a new video game they want for Christmas, they magically get an ad on their phone for that same game. Zers understand when they are being marketed to, and in turn, they have built natural immunity to various selling methods. Many traditional motivational-recruiting commercials and paid promotions on billboards or websites seem too scripted to them. Instead, candid interviews talking to celebrities with honest clips and sound bites are a much better option. This initiative should take a two-pronged approach, focusing firstly on current media celebrities with no military affiliation, and secondly on veteran celebrities who served.

The average celebrity and the average teenage influencer likely doesn't have much, if any, affiliation with the military. After all, roughly only 7% of the current U.S. adult population has served.[37] However, while these influencers' knowledge of the armed services may be very naïve, their voices and followings are solid and authentic. In addition, the most significant differentiating trend now is that they are also disaggregated and independent. With essentially costless media publishing, each influencer can produce exponentially more content quickly. Celebrities today have even more power to persuade than celebrities of the past, as they don't have some centralizing approver like a newspaper. Most of this acquired following usually comes from achievements in movies, sports, dance videos, social commentary, or other niche categories. Moreover, their followers often take direct social, moral, and behavioral advice from them when they speak genuinely.

For example, with sports, the NFL leads with the incredible job it does with its Salute to Service week. That being acknowledged, a more powerful and direct impact would be a thirty-second sound clip asking Tom Brady or Patrick Mahomes how he views those who serve. A *Military Times* reporter doing an interview would go a long way. That one clip could be shared hundreds of times on Twitter reaching thousands of Zers instantly. Having rapper Jack Harlow drop a line in a rap about the strength of our military, or influencer Addison Rae making a short dance for an upcoming military function may seem like tiny actions. Still, they would get seen by many of the eyeballs of generation Z. More than a decade ago, actors Justin Timberlake and Mila Kunis[38] were invited via social media as ball guests by enlisted Marines. Both enjoyed the spectacular event displaying military traditions and spoke publicly about it. The key point is that these mighty influencers hold the persuasion of a generation. They're better able to interact with regular people and change their lives than any commercial with special effects and loud music. Suppose the average Zer begins to see more of their peers being acknowledged by their idols for being in an organization those influencers respect. In that case, Z's inclination to at least learn more about the path to joining will increase.

The playbook of the military getting a boost in recruitment from celebrities has worked throughout history. As the U.S. restaffed its forces to compete with the Soviet Union, even the king of Rock n' Roll put on a uniform. Elvis Presley was indeed drafted, but his respect for the military and pride in serving gave young Americans an icon to look up to. He famously remarked that he felt it was a duty he had to fulfill. These celebrities joining the military ranks sends a clear signal to the young people who adore them. Additionally, famous Veterans like David Goggins, Jocko Willink, and Rob Riggle have grown to heightened popularity after their stints in service. These influencers hold powerful sway over not just the veteran communities they speak to, but also over many aspiring servicemembers. They are the prime example that you can have a great life in the military, and then use what you learned to go on to success afterward. The military will always possess a certain mystique and curiosity in the eyes of the public. The goal of these military influencers has been to shed light on the good, the bad, and the ugly features of service…something that inevitably builds more trust with listeners who are used to watching commercials of special effects dragons slayed with superhuman Soldiers.

The military needs to better connect with influencers to help augment its marketing campaigns. Generation Z is reaching the age where they are making their first major life decisions. Many will continue to use religion and the wealth of wisdom that the clergy can provide to help them carve their paths in life. However, an increasing number of Zers will be mixing religion with popular celebrity influencers. Still, some Zoomers will move away from religion entirely and adopt a more spiritual take on how to live and who to emulate.

It would behoove the services not to hire influencers or force promotional marketing, but rather to get their media corps to interact with them more. Recently, one recruiter got influencer personalities "the Island Boys" to post a pro-military recruitment shoutout on TikTok. The ingenuity of this tactic was overshadowed because the higher command quickly ordered the recruiter to remove the video. Their reasoning was that all recruiting is required to be done through government devices and not personal ones.[39] From here on, there needs to be an easy way for influencers and the DoD to interact. Establishing an influencer interface group within the Pentagon's already existing communication strategy arms would be a start. This would streamline influencer outreach and provide a repeatable process that could perpetuate continued interactions to be most effective. To begin, a detailed list of top influencers targeting military-eligible Zers should be made with the help of marketing firms, research groups, and data provided by tech platforms. Criteria for actually selecting the right influencers should focus on audience, prior messaging, and impact potential. Then the communication strategy organizations within the service branches should divide the list and begin making inroads. This new influencer interface group would lead strategy yet allow for the various press and PR corps of each branch to conduct their own outreach. Most importantly, when it comes to actually talking and putting influencer sound-bits on camera, it has to be natural and not scripted. We want more Americans hearing about the military in a natural way from their favorite celebrities. We do not want fake cameos via paid promotions that come off as government propaganda.

What needs to appear on feeds is more frank and open talk about military life from influencers. Even if some of that talk is inevitably negative, the raw truth is okay. The conversations need to be more authentic, focusing on using influencers to build trust, identity, and knowledge between Z and our nation's service branches. Service needs to be embedded as a value and a code, a way of living ingrained in our country's spiritual fabric. Just like saying grace is ingrained in its religious fabric. The military should take a hint from that young enlisted Marine who asked Mila Kunis to the ball, whose attitude was "just ask, you never know.".

In a world of information overload, reality rather than fiction is what Z wants. While the amazing *Top Gun 2* may modestly boost recruiting efforts, the DoD can't afford to rely on splashy movies depicting the most exciting parts of the job. The Navy has seemed to grasp the power of influencers with their "Sailor VS" campaign,[40] that invited famous Youtubers to compete with active-duty sailors in specific skill categories. Still, the military faces unique challenges, like the fact that commercial companies have looser data privacy and tracking restrictions than government recruiters. This blocks efficient data analysis by the military recruiting establishment as they try to identify which personalities may resonate best with their message and Z.

Some influencers like Chris Pratt, Olivia Dunne, or Mr. Beast who, on the surface, may appear to have no affiliation or interest in discussing military topics may surprise everyone with their positive thoughts on military service. Dunne recently attended a NASCAR race in Nashville and proudly posted with two Army soldiers. Those with massive followings who talk about the military or agree to take tours of bases get the reciprocal loop of being seen potentially doing exciting and interesting cameos. Think of the thousands of incredible videos that could be shot on the vast unused acreage of military bases. The DoD has one of the greatest stages ever for these influencers to perform on. By promoting their own brand simultaneously alongside the DoD's, this symbiotic relationship would benefit recruiting.

Whether from the pages of the good book or the pixels on an app, Z is looking for guidance in reflecting on what service in the modern world means to them. Utilizing influencers to help deliver this guidance into a sense of duty is an absolute must. Influencers would enable the DoD to deliver personalized messaging to differentiated pockets of Zoomers. It would help spread the messaging wider, but also stronger and more frequently due to the behavioral patterns of how Zoomers follow lifestyle influencers. However one special type of influencer has more sway over Z than any other. Next we'll examine the relationship with Z's parents and how they are crucial to figuring out the equation of recruitment.

CHAPTER 4:

Enabling Veterans to Continue to Serve

Zoomers are moving in with Boomers. In a trend that mirrors what has occurred over the past decades with our European counterparts, many young adults are moving back home with their parents. Perhaps due to the rising cost of rent or the practice being made more socially acceptable by the pandemic, parents have a more significant impact on Z than the rebellious Millennials, who would look down upon living at home. Along with this reconnection to home living comes the natural desire in any young person to please one's parents. It's human nature to want to make Mom and Dad proud, and parents often are major driving influences on young Zers' decisions. It logically tracks that to recruit more

Zoomers into the military, part of the strategy must involve persuading their parents. This monumental and life-changing decision often comes after deep, and sometimes painful, conversations with elders. A significant concern for 21st-century parents is the outcomes their children will have when joining the service. Besides safety, which is usually paramount, education and future job prospects when assimilating back into society are at the top of their mind. Only one group knows about the transformation and reintegration that encompasses an entire cycle of 21st-century service: modern Veterans. To help convince parents to support their children in joining the military, Veterans need to be inspired to transparently tell how their experiences impacted their future.

Gen Z's view of Veterans will be different than any previous generation's. As our organization retreated from touching every aspect of society, its pool of Veterans began to shrink. Now far and few to come by, Veterans are a rarity for generation Z. Additionally, those who did serve likely participated in the longest wars America has fought, and had a much higher probability of experiencing combat or multiple deployments. You're much more likely today to hear about the homeless and suicidal Veteran issues rather than the thousands of success stories that time in service enabled. An old saying proclaims that if you ask ten people about their time in the military, you will get ten starkly different opinions. While true, a few polls hold some conventional wisdom about America's newest Veterans and how the public views them. Firstly, while the Department of Veterans Affairs often gets a sour review overall, 72% of U.S. adults (on both sides of the aisle) would increase spending on Veterans.[41] In a time when trust is declining in the military as an institution, (it's at its lowest point in decades, although still higher than basically every other American institution), the general public still reports looking up to Veterans and recognizing that they have more discipline than most. When Veterans look at themselves, nearly 70% are proud of their service. Around 68% report their service as useful in getting a civilian job, but nearly half say readjusting to civilian life was difficult,[42] Sifting through these macro sentiments begins presenting a unique tapestry about Veterans today.

Firstly, the American public supports them, at least in words (unlike in some past generations). The military experience tends to be viewed favorably, with many realizing positive benefits in life post-service. "For those Veterans whose veteran status *is* well known at work, this is largely a positive thing. Six-in-ten employed Veterans whose coworkers are aware of their military service say people they interact with at work generally look up to them because of their military experience."[43] Overall, perhaps due to confirmation bias, nearly 80% of Veterans endorse joining the military, compared to only 45% of all U.S. adults. However, increasingly vocal and public stories show the difficulty that readjusting to post-military life brings. In essence, the average veteran will explain that the military gave them a great boost in life, while also having some major drawbacks. Instead of hiding this, the DoD should tap into this honesty and encourage Veterans to connect more with Gen-Z parents considering the military for their offspring. In an era where superficial advertisements follow us on devices that are always listening, honesty is a needed breath of fresh air. If a caring parent wants to know what service will be like for their child, modern Veterans are the best place to turn for the good, the bad, and the ugly truths about putting on a uniform.

If Veterans are essential in educating parents, then attention should be given to how veteran opinions can best get recorded and disseminated. Thousands of combat stories line bookstore shelves, and increasingly airtime is given to special forces operators with the most daring and exciting missions to recount. While these recountings form critical histories of our Global War on Terrorism, they often don't encompass the average expected experience for a person entering the military. Instead, a much more organized push is needed, not related to money but rather to time collecting veteran stories specifically for transparent recruiting. In an opinion piece, Marine Colonel Matthew Amidon correctly writes, "The life cycle of the all-volunteer force doesn't end with the transition to veteran status, and helping with recruitment is a new way that Veterans can serve."[44] Most Veterans would appreciate the opportunity to share their experiences from the exciting to the mundane if allowed to be honest and truthful and not forced to hold back. In essence, recruiting soon-to-be Veterans to help recruiting may prove effective.

The collection effort would be challenging for administration shops across the DoD, but they could be part of each transitioning service member's exit process. Upon separation from active duty service, each member should be mandated to give a formal, recorded, and transcribed 30-minute exit interview. The difference would be that these interviews should be explicitly focused on past experience, feedback for improving the organization, and then genuine thoughts or advice for those considering service. This final act of duty would ensure a more informed populace and enable parents of the future force to understand the nitty-gritty details better. These government documents should then be aggregated online and presented to the public for searching and viewing. Aided by analysis from A.I. natural language processing models, different topics and statistical trends will begin to emerge. Any parental searcher can have thousands of pages of perspectives in one central website to browse from. This transparent and public story-sharing helps the military improve on measuring what it provides to its people.

I created tremendous stress for my parents when I told them I was joining. Most of their fear came from lack of familiarity and simply not knowing enough about military life. Luckily a veteran played on my father's beer-league hockey team and was able to counsel him through the process. If a tool like the veteran interview database existed, many American parents would have a better starting point to learn about the life the military is selling. In business, there is a concept of a warranty, a legally binding measure of what the seller promises about the product being sold. The military is asking for so much from its servicemembers, and in turn, the product it's providing is training, a salary, and a way of life. There is never a check-up on this warranty, but collecting data on what servicemembers think after the experience is essential. If the parents of Gen Z are going to get on board with supporting military service, they should have access to as much veteran opinion as possible.

Veterans hold the examples of the past, while education is the model for the future of Gen Z. Most parents want children to get educated to better their outcomes in our country. Although there are multitudes of training schools that the military puts recruits through, society still values a traditional college program. There is a common trope from people who almost joined the military proclaiming, "I was going to serve, but my Mom wanted me to get a degree ." Veterans continuously say that their training helped them prepare for jobs in the civilian world, and numerous companies recruit Veterans solely because of their skillsets. However, many American employers don't fully equate this with a piece of paper demonstrating two or four years of civilian coursework. This perception isn't changing anytime soon and will remain an impediment for parents who want to be proud of their children while steering them down a path that yields the most success. Instead, what can change is the way the military partners with local institutions to grant official college credits. While this doesn't apply to the officer corps, who are required to have a formal, four-year degree, the 90% of servicemembers who enlist without one, would greatly benefit from closer ties to civilian academia. Currently, many military training courses give transferable credit, and some warfighters can take online courses in their free time to get degrees from participating DoD schools like National Defense University.

Additionally, the G.I. bill offers payment for college in exchange for service years, and is one of the best benefits for troops. However, more can be done to make it culturally mandated that all enlisted service members work toward some type of civilian degree while in service. Firstly, all American universities should be required by law to work with DoD personnel to understand the curriculums taught in DoD schools. These universities benefit from the safe land and free air in this country that the military provides and therefore have a duty to support it. There is nobody more deserving of colleges' knowledge than the person risking their life to defend it. They should see which pipelines match well with which degree programs and publish lists of credits issued to various occupational specialties across the military. Secondly, any remote learning platforms and courses should be opened to active-duty service members so they can enroll in night/weekend classes on their liberty time. This would be the ultimate social mobility uplifting that academia declares it wants and the military claims it provides.

A private coming from a family with no higher-level education could now freely take a high level college course online for credit in exchange for the sacrifice he/she is making. While the job of service comes first, and leisure times are few and far between in daily military life, the opening up of the ivory tower to junior enlisted Zers would be a massive signal to parents that you can get some recognized education while in uniform. This benefit would also support increased retention within the force, because fewer troops would feel the need to completely leave the military to finally get their degree. Furthermore, this external education would actually increase the ability of our people and therefore the effectiveness of our fighting force. The staff non-commissioned officer corps is the backbone of our military and the reason we are the best in the world. These competent and highly functioning individuals should be mandated to be put on a college degree track. Perhaps their length of study is 6 or 8 years rather than the traditional four, and they mix a variety of military-approved credits with local school credits along with part-time and full-time stints. Regardless, providing them the benefit and knowledge learned from college is a major key to success.

Many members of Z no longer view a few letters on a paper in highly theoretical subjects as essential to success, but the older generations still do. Most importantly, many parents still do. With more competition than ever to get admitted into universities, it doesn't look like this top-down age-based pressure will subside anytime soon. To ensure parents that the military is helping to take their children, advance them, and provide them with a better outcome when finished, education will assist in winning over their hearts and minds. Encouraging Gen Z to serve in the armed forces will require making a new and concerted outreach to their parents. Joining the military, especially when young, is an experience that changes one's life forever and impacts the entirety of the family. The best people to influence parents are their peers of similar/closer ages with military experience. With Veterans showing the transformation of past service, and education being heavily incorporated into future service, parents of Zoomers will be better able to make decisions about supporting recruits' entry into the military.

I want to take a quick moment to explain how much I owe to the Veterans I've worked with in my life. At the technology company I worked at, I got to see tremendous leaders and thinkers who used their military experience to push our economy and society forward. I will forever be grateful for them and they are one of the main forces behind my own desire to join. While they all had their struggles, they all realized that they owed the military almost as much as it owed them. I am confident that if more Zers connect to Veterans like this, we can bridge the service gap.

Ultimately though, the final decision to join will be made by signing a piece of paper in a recruiter's office. Exploring ways to better support these frontline service members in the battle for convincing Gen Z is next chapter's topic.

CHAPTER 5:
Assisting Frontline Recruiters in the Struggle

Throughout American history, there has always been some healthy tension between the young and the old. The debate about experience vs. fresh new perspectives rings more true now than in the past, because today's youth may be the first generation that is better informed than their elders. An idle young person can absorb more about the world through endless streams of podcasts, videos, and audiobooks, creating the effect of them quite literally knowing 10x more than adults at a very young age. Z, in particular, has a tougher balancing act between respect for authority and knowing simply more skills/information than Millennials or Gen X. Deciding when to listen to older people's wisdom and when to choose their own paths is a current sticking point. This paradigm hits hardest at the recruiter-recruit level.

The recruiter is the individual at the tip of the spear in the effort to bring new citizens into the military. Many describe this role as one of the hardest in the entire armed forces. To speak here as a naïve Gen-Zer who has never sat in the recruiter chair, and make direct recommendations to them specifically about the nitty gritty of their challenging job would be disingenuous. However, the fresh perspective of tying these Z trends together to reform the recruiting structure may successfully spark the proper debate. With some Zers knowing more than their older recruiters, the job has to carefully balance this trend by "keeping it real," improving recruiter training and treatment through centralization, and applying a business-minded approach.

Realism over idealism. Due to the abundance of facts and the ability to see the actual state of the world, young Zers can smell lies and tall tales exceptionally quickly. Concurrent with all of the Snapchat filters that make pictures appear better is the sense that Z can see reality and will respond negatively to false advertising. Z wants to be sold to with a "keeping it real" approach. Unfortunately, there is no shortage of Reddit posts and even viral YouTube shorts about how recruiters have outright tricked or told half-truths to Zers. Recruiters overselling military life have occurred for decades, but the quicker aggregation of knowledge on read boards lets rumors and anecdotal trends spread like wildfire. Most Zers now are just a few clicks away from encountering some of these recruiter horror stories, and just a few are enough to turn the tide in the battle for the mind of Z.

Above all, Z wants honesty, and they'll respect an honest approach that acknowledges the challenges of the military lifestyle. The collective thinking of online chat rooms is super smart and can zero in on a truth via the wisdom of crowds. The recruiting institution as a whole suffers from this bad press, likely as a result of the actions of just a few bad apples. Perception is everything for Z, and it's tough to win their trust when their guard is always up. If a recruiter gives weird vibes trying to become the bestie of a recruit, they should immediately stop because the facts are such that Zers will pick up on the farce. The previous sentence was written with Z lingo and intended to be intentionally cringey. Although Zers talk with totally different lingo, anything overdone can be seen right through by this generation.

The typical conventional answer of higher command to enabling recruitment efforts has been to encourage the overuse of online platforms by individual recruiters. While there is and should be nationally coordinated social media outreach for recruiting, individual offices making disparate posts online can send mixed messages. Instead, the continuous one-on-one contact between recruiter and recruit is likely a more impactful path as long as it's done authentically. Instead of broad postings, which should be left to national efforts, new tools like video chats to communicate face-to-face are a great use of technology to keep these links strong. Still, recruiters must respect that most Zers don't actually want any friendship lines to be crossed. Z will instead look at recruiters as elders with experience that they'll want to hear about. They'll likely consider these viewpoints along with the plethora of available open-source online research Zers tend to do. Then they will compare and mix the two to come to their own conclusion. Instead of being a connector trying to identify with Z, Z would rather have recruiters as coaches who help them navigate the decision process. As long as they don't get the sense that they're being oversold or lied to, the most real approach that reveals the recruiter's honest opinions will win the most Zers over. Only then will popular perceptions about recruiters begin to change, and Z will start to look more favorably on these now overly honest professionals.

The military promotes a decentralized command philosophy. It is one of our greatest strengths that we enable decision-making at the lowest echelons possible. This allows us to be nimble and outthink the enemy. At the same time, this decentralized culture is impeding the national recruiting effort. The lack of cross-service and cross-office collaboration is an issue. While it's true that recruiters must operate independently to correctly match the needs of the local communities they serve, they've become too separated in recent years. Whereas recruiting right now may be collocated with other service branches, the individual services have very separate messages, missions, and little cross-collaboration. Establishing an overall joint recruiting command to better centralize the messaging, training, and lifestyle treatment of recruiters would help solve this problem. This joint solution would require Congressional backing and would need each service to put aside their rivalries. While this is easier said than done, having each service compete with each other for a continually dwindling pool of recruits is a trend that needs to be reversed.

Before a Zer chooses which branch to join, they must first contemplate whether military service is right for them. This 0-to-1 decision is often where they need the most support from recruiters, and this is where the current system is breaking down. Although each branch may fight very differently, there is no reason that each branch has to recruit very differently. In business, just like the military, there is the concept of supporting and supported functions. The product the company creates is usually the core business function with management, human resources, and other categories supporting it. The service branches have to man, train, and equip, but ultimately they exist to fight adversaries and win wars. The human resource function of recruiting is not a core military competency, and almost no service members initially joined the military to do the job of recruiting. With this being the case, the branches must come together as much as possible to composite this ancillary function so that best practices are shared and disseminated. A friend of mine went to each different recruiting office and got six different answers as to why he should join the military. Sure, each branch was selling their perks but he hadn't even made the decision on uniformed service yet. I saw him coming home extremely confused, more so than before he went in to speak with recruiters. He felt that each branch was trying to put down the others. Before we fight over candidates, one centralized message about service in the first place is needed.

Recruiting jobs are notoriously challenging roles for service members to fill. In just the Marine Corps alone, the "Special Duty Assignment" data shows higher divorce rates, drug addiction rates, and a staggering number of suicides[45] among the recruiter community. Some have reported "they'd rather be in combat getting shot at than on recruiting duty" due to how hard it is with nonstop seven-day work weeks. The current problems with the recruiter lifestyle and the internal service practices that put so much pressure on "meeting mission" at all costs, drive a truly horrible culture. Mission in warfare is often life or death; when given an order, there is no backing out. In business sales, not making numbers can result in salary cuts or firing, but most good executives know that sales are a very externally dependent role. Exceptions will be made, and second chances will be given if numbers aren't hit in a particular year. Nowhere else in the DoD are future promotions, career roles, and even livelihoods tied to external factors like in recruiting. There needs to be a push to change to a "recruit the recruiter" mindset instead.

Recruiting duty needs to be seen as an honor that is highly regarded among the services and highly rewarded with less downside risk. The Army is trying to mitigate some of these current flaws. To start, they've begun by looking at sending people closer to their hometowns in the hopes that they can better connect with where they're from. They are also even considering performance-based pay to reward this complicated job. On the less material side, there are reports that they are coming out with a new medal for those that convince someone else to join. While everyone appreciates some chest candy, "the majority of the recruiters reported that each of these awards is only sometimes-to-never motivating as an incentive[46]". More than all of this, training needs to be done differently. Just like how recruiters need to "coach" rather than persuade Zers to gain their trust, coaching recruiters themselves down a knowledge discovery pathway must occur.

This difficult role can't be one where you're simply thrown in the fire and learn "on the job." That makes each recruiter too variable and too impacted by the styles of the older recruiters at a station. Part of this journey must include enabling recruiters with large, centralized data tools. A 2019 RAND study surveyed experts who reported that, "taking better advantage of third-party data and integrating it with their first-party data could enrich their marketing and recruiting operations." Accompanying the need for better information is the need for better analytical tools. With the already restricted data that the DoD is able to acquire, the right people must be given the right programs to use that data. Recruiters reported that the tools available to them "did not prioritize individuals, leads, activities, or events based on their return on investment."[47] Interbranch recruiting practices and data need to be shared. A massive data push into recruiting should be organized jointly with all the recruiting commands working top-down to bring in the right people who are trained properly.

The recruiting job is the ultimate sales role. It's one of the most challenging types of sales because the thing being sold is a significant life change and an irreversible experience. Looking to the business world with far superior data and sales methods would be a great way to grow recruiters' skill sets. Hamstringing recruiters by not giving them access to the most up-to-date thinking and training will never work to close this gap. Recruiting should be afforded the best resources the civilian world has to offer. Technical training like the powerful LinkedIn recruiting software should be made available, and recruiters should have access to more business sales resources and books. Recruiters selected for duty must be given formal sales training even before ever attending one of the service recruiting schools.

Recruiters need to be taught to think in an often non-military mindset. Barring an occasional consultant report that may make its way to some random DoD office, most recruiters have probably never employed a fundamental business framework like Porter's five forces[48]. This one framework on competitive strategy would have recruiters looking at the 1. Threat of new entrants, 2. Threat of substitutes, 3. Competitors, 4. Power of suppliers, and 5. Power of buyers, when it comes to the lifestyle they're selling to Gen Zers. A simple note card that could be filled out in a quick session would enable recruiters to better frame how they sell the physical social network that is the military. This is especially handy when persuading recruits against competing job offers.

Other helpful tools to grow a recruiter's mind would be analyzing CAC or customer acquisition costs to better determine how many resources to allocate to particular recruits. Say a perfect recruit on paper has a super high impediment in their mental propensity to joining. It may be too costly in recruiter time to try and chase after them. These are just a few strategic-level frameworks that recruiting command should agree on and then push down to the tactical-level recruiters. They must support thinking bigger and clearer about their approaches, rather than getting sucked so deep into the stress and grind of every day phone calls to high school kids.

With that, local high schools should be compelled to assist with some of this. Thomas Spoehr writes for the Heritage foundation that, "due to burdensome laws and outdated policies, military recruiters are often forced to "cold call" candidates, using unrefined lists of high school students."[49] While high schools shouldn't become geared to military recruiting, bringing back a half-semester civics curriculum could help. Even incorporating a nationally-approved military studies package as part of American history classes would certainly assist in educating youth with a baseline military knowledge. This would significantly lower the familiarity barrier that these recruiters are faced with. It would reduce the "CAC" in terms of the educational time these recruiters spend just talking about what the military does, thus enabling a slightly easier overall sales process.

Standing in front of a Zer who may have more knowledge and skills, and trying to convince them to join the armed services in today's age is an extremely daunting task. The brave few recruiters who keep the force alive do an incredible job as it is. However, the trends are making this job more and more challenging each year. The DoD will have to combine a centralized and data-driven approach. Apart from simply increasing the number of recruiters and allocating more manpower to that profession, this may be the only "magic bullet" available. Over time, the DOD must better train recruiters to employ modern business sales tactics to "keep it real", and coach Zoomers on their military journey.

However, making contact with a recruit is only the first step. Even if a recruiter successfully persuades them into joining, they are then faced with another major hurdle. Getting past the qualifications process is more difficult than ever with the new digital health system that is the focus of the next chapter.

CHAPTER 6:

Modernizing the Health Accession System

The military stands out from other sectors of society in that its work often has some physical component. While increasingly more jobs require little to no daily physical activity, each service branch still mandates a baseline level of health standards to complete its mission. One of the "big four" disqualifiers for potential Gen Z recruits is due to health considerations. Certain officials can use this as a cover when putting the blame back on the youth for not being up to recruitable standards. What is actually going on when people give these inflated numbers of "Americans unfit for service" is a classic example from the famous 1954 book by Darell Huff titled "How to Lie with Statistics."[50]

Generation Z is no more unhealthy than Boomers, Millennials, or the Greatest Generation that won WWII. Instead, our healthcare and digital record tracking improvements have wholly detached the military performance goals we aim for from the statistical ground truth that the data represents. Overall, Gen Z has similar, if not better, physical health profiles than past generations, yet ridiculous medical standards prevent many from joining. From the nonsensical disqualifiers like eczema and flat feet to the more severe like spinal curvature, these outdated rules need to be analyzed by new healthcare professionals. The entire health waiver process needs to be redone, focusing only on if service members are physically able to do their future job or not.

Behold the largest change to military healthcare in the 21st century: Military Health System Genesis. Genesis is a massive new undertaking that digitizes all civilian and military health records. Despite the many problems with the actual Genesis software itself,[51] The noble aspiration to go paperless is an excellent DoD initiative to modernize and create efficiency. However, this quickly became an example of speedy technology outpacing sluggish human policy. The name Genesis is quite ironic because it essentially allows the military to see an applicant's entire medical history…all the way back to his/her birth. What this has then caused is a massive increase in the amount of medical filing needed for waivers. If every little doctor visit, bone fracture, and allergic reaction is now documented and in the system, applicants are forced to disclose and get proper approval for minor health incidents that in the past were ignored. It's long been known that recruiters have encouraged recruits to lie about medical histories, and while that is a bad practice in theory, it's not always bad in reality. Most Americans will have some minor medical blip from their past that has absolutely no impact on them and wouldn't reduce their performance in uniform.

Now, if you so much as sought out a medical professional's opinion after a slight bump on the head during sports, you have to go back to a litany of doctors to prove you didn't have a concussion or that you are no longer impacted by it. Only then can you hope and pray to receive a medical waiver to join. Through Genesis, we removed the messy but perhaps more effective frontline discretion from recruiters and put it into an all-seeing software system. From a historical perspective, we may not have ever seen some of our greatest leaders put on a uniform. President John F. Kennedy was rejected by both the Army and the Navy due to his various illnesses before he eventually served honorably. If Genesis were around, then he'd have no shot of ever making it past the recruiting station. Perhaps the Cuban Missile Crisis would've gone differently.

This current debacle is an excellent display of misaligned incentives and broad-stroke policies that fail their objectives. From a first and immediate-order perspective, the military wants healthy Gen Zers who don't have underlying medical conditions that would prevent them from doing their job or cause undue risk to themselves or others. From a secondary and future perspective, the military doesn't want to end up paying VA claims and supporting every medical issue veterans face if that issue wasn't related to their time in service. While there have been terrible cases of VA fraud that have undoubtedly hurt the American taxpayer, those people are outliers who don't comprise the general spirit of the brave few who choose to put on a uniform. Much more common is that throughout their lives, Americans will need medical care just by nature of our modern lifestyles.

Whether it be one year or twenty, time in the military will inevitably increase the amount of healing needed. As we practically beg our next generation to make that trade-off and try to explain to them that 40% of your pay is future VA health benefits/ongoing care, it's silly to then have such an aversive national attitude to one day paying for that care. It's equivalent to promising social security benefits all one's life and then taking away that benefit upon retirement after forty years in the work-force. Forcing one to go through incredible detail, running from doctor to doctor to document which injury was related to your years in service and which wasn't, lessens the pool of future recruits. If society wants to support veterans, it must accept that continued medical support is prob-ably the biggest and most direct way to do just that. Either we collectively agree conceptually and in practice that once you put on a uniform, you will have your future health ills covered, or we might as well throw out the concept of veteran health support. Denying young patriots the chance to serve in uniform because of the fear that some past illness will let them claim more VA benefits in the future is a terrible signal to send to those we are potentially asking to protect us.

Admittedly, this is one the most nuanced and difficult issues in this book. For one, the fiscal state of the U.S. is in such dire straits that more efficient budgeting is a must if we're to survive as a nation. VA healthcare benefits have risen dramatically over the past decades. As the country's older veterans continue to age, these costs will only increase. My grandfather at 17 enlisted as a gunner in an SBD-Dauntless in the Pacific. He served heroically in WWII, lived an amazing life, and when he was facing dementia in his final years, we were able to put him into a terrific VA nursing home. On principle, we can all agree that those who made such sacrifices deserve care from our society no matter the cost. In reality though, there is going to have to be some serious austerity measures in all government departments, and VA healthcare won't be spared. My point here is that the issue of VA health spending needs to be solved on the backend, after years of service, not on the frontend as a way of disqualifying potential recruits. We'll never have a perfect system, but if the fear of future costs create such a Draconian accession pipeline, we'll never be able to meet recruiting goals.

The real emphasis on military-entrance health processing should be focused only on actual job impacts. The medical standard needs to be revised to determine if it serves the intentions behind it. Investigating whether or not a Zer had a broken arm in fourth grade and then requiring a waiver for those that did is utterly ridiculous. Ninety-nine percent of the time, someone had a broken bone like that as a child, and they recovered completely fine. Currently, the military can disqualify an applicant for many issues that would be impossible to say actually reduces combat effectiveness. Does a tree nut allergy disqualify an administration clerk sitting at a desk in the Pentagon? Does an aircraft mechanic need to have a history of zero prescribed medications? This lag time that recruits spend running around to doctors is dangerous in that many may be scared away by their first encounter with military bureaucracy. Zers will wonder if it takes this much red-tape cutting just to join this organization, then what culture exists once they are inside and a part of it? The new system has added so much uncertainty that it has created an "unpredictable process for recruits that last weeks — sometimes months — longer than it did before Genesis came online."[52] For those enlisted recruits that have specifically contracted jobs, there should be specifically laid-out medical disqualifiers that require more follow-up. If a future pararescue diver has civilian health injuries in their file, then it is logical that they should be required to get waivers due to the physical nature of diving. Conversely, if a future cook had some dental visits during childhood, then the DoD job requirement standard should automatically allow doctors to ignore those records.

Not only should specific jobs have specific medical inspection strings attached to them, but the severity of increasingly common medical issues needs to be reconsidered. Gen Z has access to better and more abundant health care than any generation before. While massive issues and disparities may still exist in child and teen care in the United States, overall, Z can see more doctors in more locations for better pricing than in the past. With that has come increased and sometimes over-prescription of various medicines. Particularly, "focus drugs" like Adderall have seen rapid usage in the past years to combat ADHD. While it's not the military's job to opine on proper drug dosage in today's youth, it can recognize that the skyrocketing of this trend shouldn't necessarily disqualify these individuals from service. Similar to a point-based system, it would make more sense for the military to analyze the amount and frequency of study drug usage. Prescribed use over a three-year period that then ended is a lot different than a ten-year, high-dosage intervention that is ongoing. This level of detail matters and must be adjudicated before the recruit tries to get their packet over the finish line.

As a corollary to this, popular generation Z culture promotes exceptionally health-conscious lifestyles. One criticism other generations can accurately lob against us is that we are too concerned with wellness. We're not only more likely to go to a doctor, but we're also more likely to demand health and wellness be a part of everyday workplace discussions. Z has proliferated the usage of tech-enabled "wearable" devices like the Oura ring and the Fitbit bracelet. Z is obsessed with veganism, green juices, and plant-based meat products. We're watching what we eat and where it is sourced from on a whole new level. The total eligible/qualified recruit pool of Americans is likely substantially higher if you make the health standards logical and keep them at what they've been in the past. The military has operated just fine for years with the same baseline American health when paper records were the norm. Sure, this led some recruiters and recruits to be the objective arbiters of medical readiness rather than what the civilian health records showed, but it allowed a much larger pool of people to pull from.

What's occurring here is the "bystander effect" at its maximum. The bystander effect is exemplified when a significant group witnesses a problem but assumes everyone else will solve it, so they choose not to intervene. It was first described in psychology during the tragic murder of Kitty Genovese, which likely happened with as many as 12 people listening or being able to take action. Each service knows the new health system combined with the old standards will massively rupture recruiting. Decision makers in Congress and higher commands understand the problem but believe it falls into someone else's court to undergo the laborious process of rewriting more specific instructions for health codification.

So, in the end, the next JFK may get turned away because of an obscure medical visit they had in middle school. Overall, the waiver/health approval process should be deeply analytical and based on data. Perhaps if studies show that right-side ACL tears during childhood lead to significantly worse servicemember run performance, then that indicator will need a unique investigation for approval. Right now, everyone's go-to answer is just "oh, well they can get a waiver for that.". The waiver process is long, is often arbitrary, and risks discouraging recruits in the process. We can't allow a broken system to continue on the hope that making frequent exceptions to it is the way forward.

Objectively in most cases, past medical occurrences will likely not affect actual job performance. The large DoD health organization successfully proved it could overhaul legacy systems and bring new digital-records technology. If it can do that, it can also overhaul legacy policy to adapt to the new generation. The software behind Genesis itself is not the problem. The actual concept of the system is fine, but the ancient regulations it enforces are where the pain point is. The Department of Defense Instruction 6130.03 (commonly called the "DODI") is the policy that needs to change. The entire document needs to be carefully reexamined, amended, and republished. That is where the work needs to be done.

Allowing those with tree-nut allergies to serve in the military isn't going to lower our standards. Instead, each department health service needs to sit down with medical professionals from around the US to come up with a new and objective list of medical disqualifiers for each unique MOS. Then, better job matching can be made and more individuals can make it through the entry-level screening process. Then, the DODI will stop crippling the force.

A more pragmatic approach to determining if past medical history actually impacts job performance will see recruiting eligibility skyrocket. With that, we close out the discussion on recruiting fundamentals and turn to Part 2 of the book. There we'll analyze Gen Z's expectations for a modern workplace and reforming the DoD to be more in line with that.

PART II
WORKFORCE PARITY:
Bringing Military Working Conditions In Line With Gen Z Expectations of The Modern Civilian Workplace

My first official summer job was in a human-grade dog-food factory. The factory work inspired a great pride in me for made-in-America items as well as for the value of actually producing goods. At the same time, the neglected manufacturing sector that was hit massively during the great financial crisis remains one of the essential staples of our nation's future progress and success. The assembly line we set up was rather basic and comprised of two "fulfillment" associates, one manager, and myself. On the very first day, I saw the stark contrast between the younger generation and the older Gen X. As we sat down for our lunch break, trying to ignore the continuous scent of dog food mix, I learned their different career progression philosophies. The forty-five-year-old had worked in factories his whole life, detailing how he often stayed in the same buildings when one company was sold to another and changed its name/product. He explained that in 2008 many companies closed down, but if the factory lights stayed on, then he'd remain hopeful that a new company would buy up the production. The 21-year-old had already been an Uber driver and Door Dasher, and had plans to move from this factory job to a job in medical device sales in just two short years. Their differing philosophies had no actual impact on their job performance. They both could box an order in about 3 minutes, while it took my clumsy hands a whopping 5. However, I began to see the new views of those who came of working age post the major financial meltdown.

Part two discusses key expectations that Gen Z has for the modern workplace. While not everywhere can be like a Silicon Valley oasis with kombucha on tap and comfy lounge chairs, Zoomers expect much more from their employers than in the past. Military life and the jobs those in uniform are expected to do will always be inherently different than most civilian sector employment. However, the following chapters remark on how some basic improvements around pay type, promotion speed, reskilling, and mobile work can propel the DoD into creating a more level playing field.

CHAPTER 7:
Paying for Performance

Money is often the most controversial topic in military affairs. While crafting the world's largest defense budget, America's politicians are planning to spend $857.9 billion in the 2023 National Defense Authorization Act.[53] With such a large number, it's daunting to imagine the thousands of accounting lines these dollars eventually funnel into. Hundreds of books and speakers have opined on defense spending, and many of the recruitment problems facing the military could easily be hand-waved with more money. However, the nation must stay fiscally responsible and we're running out of money to spend. Instead of just "throwing more money" at these recruitment issues, the premise the Armed Forces must operate under is that they will have to make do with less. They must assume they won't be able to spend a single dollar more on recruitment, but instead have to work harder and smarter with what they've been allocated. The military way of dealing with large war campaigns is to break things down to the strategic, operational, and tactical (SOT) levels. This strong framework is perfect for planning to tackle defense budgeting.

The strategic level concerns Generals and Congress, the topline numbers that go into major line items like how much each service branch is budgeted annually. The operational level is where each service branch invests in key weapons programs, training initiatives, and their yearly goals for manning and equipping troops. The rubber meets the road at the tactical level, and financial decisions here can most directly impact current and prospective military individuals. The financial item most significantly tied to recruitment is naturally base pay. Military base pay is an extremely complex bureaucratic system that doesn't lend itself well to serving modern-day recruiting. This chapter focuses on understanding how pay in the military is incongruous with Generation Z, and proposes that shaping a better performance-based rewards system will incentivize more recruits.

Generation Z is deeply concerned with their finances, even more than past generations. The World Economic Forum published an article titled "Why Generation Z has a totally different approach to money."[54]. It explains that Z is unique in its fiscal approaches compared to previous generations. Since Zoomers watched their Gen X parents lose nearly half their median net worth in the Great Financial Crisis, they want jobs with security. They're willing to work evenings and weekends in non-traditional schedules. Similarly, the Deloitte 2022 Gen Z survey shows the cost of living as the number one widespread concern.[55] Z cares deeply about how much they are getting paid, who they are getting paid by, and what actions they are getting paid for. With the global macro economy on shaky ground, the argument could be made that this money anxiety is due to recent trends. However, these young adult payment issues have been bubbling up for years. Georgetown University's Center on Education and the Workforce published a study explaining that besides young adults (ages 22-27) who have graduate and professional degrees, "All other groups of young adults have lower employment rates now than similarly educated young adults did in 2000."[56]

The current military pay situation is arguably worse for young servicemembers than for their peers in the private sector. While rational economic theory holds that wages are "sticky" and don't adjust immediately for inflation, they do end up adjusting over time. The military only gets a basic pay bump yearly when Congress passes the NDAA. This year's 4.6% pay raise is being advertised as the largest pay bump in two decades, but as it misses the fact that since inflation is over 7%,[57] this effectively serves as a cut to real military wages. The question to ask is how service branches can most effectively attract top talent and reward behaviors that support the completion of the mission in the face of intense competition from civilian employers. Performance is one compensation area that the DoD can focus on to persuade more potential joiners from Gen Z to look at military pay in a better light.

Performance-based pay is a superior method for motivating Americans to join the military. Generation Z has watched their peers get extremely wealthy through non-traditional "side hustles" and online videos. Teenage Tik-Tok sensation Charli D'Amelio is estimated to be worth millions and makes more in one post than most Americans do each day. The whopping sums that brands are paying her are because she is one of the world's most popular teenage social-media marketers. She has "won the competition" in a sense, and she, therefore, gets paid more than someone with far fewer followers. Generation Z understands these

WE DON'T WANT YOU, UNCLE SAM

principles and wants opportunities to be rewarded for more challenging, superior work that makes an individual or a team stand out.

This trend is only going to increase. With the onset of large language models like ChatGPT-3, Zers have more technological leverage at their disposal than all of NASA did in the 1960s. Zers will continue to produce and innovate, but those taking advantage of AI will literally be able to start businesses and trends at speeds never before seen. This will inevitably create more winners who are paid for their creations. Those that put in the work will be rewarded and with such ease of access to these tools, it will be hard for Zers to pick careers where they can't benefit from them. Standardized military pay currently allows for nearly no deviation; those doing "better" work aren't rewarded in their checking accounts.

The leading economist studying military recruiting is Beth Asch of the RAND Institute. In one of her papers, "Military and Civilian Pay Levels, Trends, and Recruit Quality,"[58] Asch uses regression analysis to prove that as military pay rose service-wide compared to civilian pay, recruit quality rose in three of the four largest service branches. This is a logical and obvious conclusion, but the Army stood as an outlier with a slight downward trend. The Army's unique pay structure may yield some answers when analyzing the results. Of the branches, the Army relies heaviest on bonuses. Bonuses in the military are currently paid based on actions, and the following is a list of various bonuses recruiters currently advertise on the Army's recruiting website: job signing bonus, active army enlistment bonus, and quick ship bonus. Another paper by Asch shows that even when doubling the average enlistment bonus (100% jump), the number of high-quality enlistments would only rise by 4-17% at most[59]. Performance bonuses are different. Performance bonuses reward successful results; they offer the ability to achieve more once in the military. Performance bonuses could be structured like investment and consulting firms offering junior analysts their yearly pay. There is a bonus pool for the unit and the individual. If the unit or team hits specific objective goals compared to other units, that unit would be awarded a larger bonus pool. The unit's commanding officer would then have the discretion to award various individual members of the team performance-related bonuses.

Charlie Munger's famous quote, "Show me the incentives and I'll show you the outcome" rings true here. If you incentivize superior performance, then you will get superior performance. Heroic operational valor is one thing. However, we'd be naive to think that most people are willing to continuously go above and beyond during mundane days in garrison. I recall back in high school when there would be a graded vs. an ungraded assignment. If it was graded, everyone would grind hard to get a high mark. Ungraded assignments often came in half-complete and certainly not 100% correct. Like it or not, humans have been and will always have some monetary motivation since it is one of the easiest stores of societal value. "Grades" in the adult world are money and besides punishment, it's probably the single best way to motivate a group of young, Gen-Z servicemembers to put in extra effort.

The Sergeant Major of the Army has even hinted at interest in setting up pilot programs to explore the idea.[60] The new performance pay and standards for awarding it should also be public and should not make up more than 10% of a junior enlistee's or junior officer's base pay. Since the program's goal is to increase recruitment at the lower ranks, this should only be implemented for entry-level officers and entry-level enlisted (perhaps those who have been in the military for four years or less). Equal pay raises across ranks are the most expensive and cost-ineffective way to increase recruitment. One-time, bonus-like performance pay will provide a sought-after upside. Giving young recruits agency over their income will be a powerful attractor. In an age where "equity" and ownership, as opposed to basic salaries, are seen as the way to build wealth, having your paycheck tied in part to your productivity will be a motivating factor for new recruits to consider.

For as long as the military has existed, it has needed to pay its members. Base pay provides money into troops' bank accounts, but a more modern system that rewarded high performers would be desirable to generation Z. At its core; it would provide a plan for a system that promoted more optionality and freedom. Related to money is time, and Z places a huge premium on it. Next we'll explore how service contracts can be modified to fall in line with Z's timelines.

CHAPTER 8:
Improving Service To Fit Modern Timelines

C areer patterns are changing. The typical trajectory of staying at one company for decades has declined since the turn of the century. Young Zers no longer talk about four to five years on the job, they're switching as much as every two years. The Bureau of Labor Statistics reports that "the median tenure of workers ages 55 to 64 (9.8 years) was more than three times that of workers ages 25 to 34 years (2.8 years).[61] From a consistency standpoint, the four years as a high school student may be the longest-tenured position that Zers ever hold. Karin Kimbrough, the chief economist at LinkedIn, said in a statement that "it's normal for career starters to be in an experimental phase where they're still figuring out what they want out of a job, and aren't always ready and willing to settle[62]". This sets the generation up with major commitment issues that are directly at odds with the nature of current military contracts. Generally speaking, the standard military contract requires four years of active duty and some portion in the reserves. Although nuances exist, nearly all contracts have an eight-year "total commitment" to the force. Just the concept of eight years to the average 18-year-old Zoomer is frightening. Overall, Z places a massive emphasis on optionality. They want to keep up with the fast-moving information age and progress at a much quicker rate than their ancestors. There is a huge premium placed on speed and time. The military must keep up with this and satisfy the dilemma of the clock.

Foreign allies may hold the answer regarding service length. We'd be foolish not to occasionally acknowledge some of the techniques, tactics, and procedures other militaries employ that are particularly effective. Contracts are one of those categories. While it may be shocking to the average American, nearly 50 sovereign nations still have some form of compulsory military service. Two of our strongest allies in the world to further examine are South Korea and Israel. Both of these nation-states have incredibly hostile neighbors, and the need for a warrior population to defend themselves is critical. Both nations have significantly shorter service requirements than the U.S. The Israeli Defense Forces require 32 months for males and 24 for females, while the Republic of Korea Army differs by branch but is generally 18 months for males. Both militaries sometimes increase time requirements slightly for specialized jobs. (Pilots in all nations typically have much longer requirements due to their extensive flight training.) Still, they take a much more detailed and nuanced approach matching the job category with the time they need to actually be in uniform. The U.S. should heed this example and do the same. To quote the famous movie line and now a meme, "four-year contracts are so last year's trend." They are extremely out of fashion for a group of Zers who want to experience being in service while keeping one foot still in the civilian world. These shorter contracts don't have to be as ubiquitous as the standard four-year terms; they could even be highly competitive for select spots only. Overall though, more of them should exist.

There is a solid counterargument to be made that the military wouldn't be getting the proper return on investment that it puts into training, if troops can come and go quickly in this revolving door setup. A more robust counter to that counter would be to ask the Ukrainians if they'd want more people trained up when February 2022 came around. Regardless of whether those people were doctors, chefs, or school teachers, they'd be much more effective assets having even just a few months of a training head start. In the end, our military doesn't fight with masks on. Unlike some adversaries, we show our faces with pride, and part of that pride is knowing that we can quickly enjoy the fruits of the prosperous, democratic economy we are working to defend. Allowing Zoomers to dip in and out of that at a quicker pace won't yield a less capable force.

The other part of the equation regarding time is the ability for Zoomers to change course and quit when a job isn't working out. One predominant phenomenon that followed the work-from-home explosion has been the concept of quiet quitting. From adults who have been in the labor force for decades to first-job Zers, many have simply been putting in the minimum effort to get by or have resigned entirely from jobs they no longer want to deal with. Quiet quitting and the great resignation have shown Z the power the modern worker has. The military doesn't have any room for behavior like this, and with a mission predicated on life or death, it can't afford to have its warfighters simply refuse to do work.

Believe it or not, the military is facing its own challenges in dealing with this problem. Dubbed "ROAD" by enlisted personnel, being "retired on active duty" is when someone basically gives up and barely does what is required. Unlike in the corporate world, where you can incentivize people back into action with the carrot, the military currently solely relies on the stick. Threatening and enacting punishment can only go so far if no active regulations are broken. Some quiet quitters in the military are careful not to get in trouble but still barely contribute because they no longer feel aligned with the mission, but have to ride out their contract. The fundamental difference between the private sector and the military here is that civilian Zoomers can "quiet quit" or resign from one job, and move on to the next with relative ease. Military personnel who sign formal contracts with the government don't have that luxury. Instead, they are threatened with general or less than honorable discharge. The administrative paperwork to separate someone for cause is such a bureaucratic burden that it is nearly impossible to do, barring some actual criminal offenses.

If a Zoomer who joined the military were to express interest in leaving it early, they'd inevitably hear the oft-repeated phrase, "you signed a contract". *De jure* contracts that forcibly bind Zoomers to a cause for fear of negative future repercussions are a major turn-off for many. The truth is that one deals with tremendous uncertainty when researching and ultimately deciding to join the military. A decision is made with hopefully the right intentions, but things change over the course of a year, and forcing such a stern long-term commitment is akin to imprisonment. In addition to the honorable, generable, and less-than-honorable discharges currently available, there should be a new category for those who quit after a short service period. While they shouldn't be allowed to waltz back into society unscathed, they shouldn't have a looming record over their head that prevents them from many future job opportunities.

Instead, there should be a new contracted option allowing for a 1-2 year evaluation period. It would consist of satisfactorily completing all training and at least one half-year billet. Similar to how evaluations, dubbed Fitreps in the Navy and Enlisted Evaluation Reports in the Army, already occur in the military, a new recruit would be screened and counseled. If that newly enlisted service member was totally failing to adapt and simply was a drag on the unit due to lack of effort, there would be a proper pathway toward removing them from service. After this, that person can be released to specific community-service jobs that tangentially support the military and its local communities. Working at the gas station on base without receiving military benefits would legitimately provide more cost-benefit value for the DoD than someone "quiet quitting" in an active duty unit. Basically this path allows for "firing" without destroying someone's future.

This new category of regular discharges would require modifications to contracts, but it would also enable a better allocation of manpower to socially net-positive organizations. Suppose wearing the uniform became too much for a Zoomer, and they hated their existence and were unwilling to contribute, even after working with command and looking at unit transfers. In that case, they should have the option to serve their communities in a more civilian capacity. This also goes for the many edge cases of prolonged injuries or pending court actions. Instead of putting these groups of people on random details and useless tasks, they should be required to serve in their community allowing the country to get a return on investment for their training time. This "testing the waters" option will enable Zoomers to treat potential service like they would other career opportunities with internships or probationary hiring periods.

The final area where the military can bend time to Z's needs is faster or varied career promotions. Slowing promotions to a very orderly time-in-grade system may allow the masses to move at a predictable pace, but certain high achievers will look to other organizations before joining one where they can't advance any quicker based on achievement. Overhauling the system for everyone is too tricky, but quick hot-fill billeting when a need arises in the active component is an excellent opportunity to push certain people ahead. More hot-fill billets should be offered in the active forces,, and specific ones should be denoted to increase the speed of promotion. If doing job x becomes important and immediately needed, it would be a massive carrot to dangle if a quicker promotion resulted from volunteering for it.

High achievers would be drawn to this competitive system. In the private sector, even at the lower entry levels, there are still some fast tracks to promotion. The military very rarely early promotes junior enlisted servicemembers. This helps the average because, barring some negative feedback or legal issues, you have the security of promotion to the next rank after putting in your time. Inevitably this also helps the lowest performers move ahead. By doing this and allowing the whole entry cohort to promote at the same pace for the first few years, you hamstring the higher performers who could likely do a higher-ranking job sooner and should be incentivized to want to. Faster promotions, or a better way to say it is varied promotions based on performance for the higher achievers, would also more quickly satisfy the general Z need for continuous career switching.

Since time will continue to tick faster and faster, Zoomers want to understandably zoom ahead. Locking themselves into long-term commitments at such a young age is not interesting for many. To prepare for this, the military should take a more nuanced approach when dealing with service contracts. For one, it should consider offering more short-term contracts like many of our foreign allies do. In addition, different job categories should have different contract lengths. The current distinctions are made for only a few jobs, whereas they should occur on a much more granular level. Moreover, a new opt-out option should be implemented to deal with those that determine that military life is not working for them. The ability to transfer over to a community service role would likely provide more benefit to society while also increasing the number of young Americans with at least some basic military training. Lastly, hot-fill billeting, allowing for faster career progression, should entice certain Z strivers to join due to less rigid time-in-grade requirements and structures. The paradigm of time has always been crucial in warfare, and with the modern battlefield occurring in recruiting offices, it cannot be overlooked.

While Zoomers often consider time when they sign up for jobs, they are also conscious of the overall state of the economy. Economic swings between booms and busts have massive impacts on military recruiting. Examining how smoothing out recruiting so that it is resilient in both times of low and high unemployment will be the focus of the following pages.

CHAPTER 9:

Smoothing Out Economic Cycles

The larger macroeconomic cycle is going to have an impact on every industry. The military, being a government organization that must always be on call, is actually countercyclical to prevailing hiring trends. For one, it's reasonable to say that the world gets more unstable during economic crashes as the potential for conflict rises, thus encouraging increased spending on the military. More than that, when other companies freeze hiring and shut their doors to new graduates, the military becomes a much more attractive option with its pay guarantee and stable job. For years, recruiters have battled the federal reserve while trying to maintain balanced numbers throughout the whole cycle. Current estimates have that a 10% decrease in civilian unemployment reduces the number of qualified recruits by upwards of 4%.[63]

While joining the military isn't often done to make money, relative economic progress and social standing matter. Contrary to popular perception, the military is firmly made up of the middle class of Americans. Among enlisted recruits, the middle three income quintiles are overrepresented, and the top and bottom quintiles are underrepresented[64]. Putting this together, the military's recruiting focus logically attracts the middle class and should ideally be able to maintain that middle-class lifestyle during and post-service. In the end, the economic impact of recessions and boom cycles on joining the military makes recruitment too cyclical. Military recruitment needs to be detached from economic cycles by promoting side hustles and explaining pay in ways that are similar to other jobs.

Zoomers are part of the content generation, and they love content creation. The cost to broadcast a trend, idea, or dance has fallen dramatically, enabling everyone to be their own producer. For the first time in history, we've broken past strong institutions that exercise thought control. The new ability to express opinions and create content for others is a massive money making opportunity. The previously mentioned gig economy, which has seen many Zers become self-employed Uber drivers, Door Dashers, and online task fillers provides many with much-needed secondary income. The military should capitalize on this trend and allow for "side hustles," even going so far as to promote them. Stepping back, it's crucial to analyze the landscape for side jobs in the military. For decades now, getting a secondary income stream needs to be approved by your chain of command and is generally a frowned-upon practice in the institution. Three main reasons exist for this. Firstly, the military is like an emergency room doctor. You are required to technically always be on duty and ready to spring into action at a moment's notice. This is a weak argument with the current way that wars are fought. While specific units that are forward deployed are indeed always ready to go, and particular jobs in certain career fields monitor live threats 24/7, the average service member would have days to weeks to prepare before actually going to an emergency battle.

It would be a truly rare contingency to have a private recalled immediately from whatever side hustle they were doing and ordered to pack their bags to be overseas in 24 hours. Secondly, there is a legitimate safety risk that if people work two jobs, they may be more exhausted and less able to perform their potentially dangerous military job the next day. This is a fair consideration, but the nature of Gen Z's side hustles largely nullifies this. Z isn't running out to swing a pickaxe in a coal mine. The vast majority are likely posting videos online, trading cryptocurrency, or fulfilling short digital tasks. Exhaustion from these activities is unlikely and is undoubtedly less fatigue-inducing than having to change diapers while raising kids, as most of the more seasoned enlisted force is dealing with.

There also exists the fear that if you do one of these things on the side, you're not "all-in." It's not fair to equate one leisure activity as more societally important or acceptable than another one just because the second activity makes some money. It is true that context switching drops productivity. Multitasking is essentially a myth, with science proving that only 2.5% of the population can effectively do it.[65] So the force should be wary if, at their current job post, a servicemember was checking their Amazon sales account during lunch breaks. However, setting up agreed-upon boundaries and only allowing secured liberty time to work on the side hustle would effectively deal with this. Finally, the last point against allowing side jobs are the ethical violations they may raise. Serving in uniform is not meant for profit but is, by nature, an act of sacrifice to support the greater society. Service should not be done to enrich oneself, and even posting videos in uniform can be seen as profiteering from the good brand it represents.

Nonetheless, the average new recruit isn't subject to such stringent ethical issues and isn't in danger of making a worldly impact via an alternative income stream. A corporal who posts her twitch video game stream to a community of followers for a few dollars isn't upsetting the international order. That same corporal may have just been able to buy her partner a nice dinner that week because of that activity, which may have made an enormous difference in the happiness of his/her life. In essence, there is no good reason the military shouldn't support its troops in becoming more financially independent, and taking on some extra productive tasks during downtime. Battalion commanders should go so far as to promote side hustles and ensure their troops have knowledge about how to acquire extra income. This trend helps make the military similar to civilian life and breaks down the strange barrier that exists between those working in uniform and those working in the regular world. There should be read-boards on bases allowing new joiners to know what possible side gigs others are up to. Informal chats with superiors about advice and text message groups for various categories should be promoted to enable more to get in on the action. This initiative would improve the spending power of servicemembers, and allow potential recruits who have been doing this type of work before they joined to continue even while in uniform.

A cost-free move that would make military pay similar to civilian jobs would be to switch to a salary system. Instead of increasing pay, reducing the shielding around it may be exactly what is needed to entice Zers to be able to compare the military to the civilian sector. Currently, a large part of military pay comes in the form of benefits. While benefits like free lodging, subsidized food, and lower tax brackets on deployment are great, they don't always translate 1:1 in the mind of a Zoomer. The Congressional Budget Office led a non-partisan study of military pay and found that cash pay (which comprises basic pay, food and housing allowances, and tax advantages) only accounts for a little more than half of total pay.[66] The other part of this comes from active-duty healthcare, retirement healthcare, and post-service VA and retirement benefits. A major issue with this is that most service members leave after their first enlistment contract, and they never receive the retirement benefits that are calculated in the formula.

In addition, even if they may realize the benefit of free healthcare when they go to the clinic, they seldom will calculate in their head that "Hey, I just saved $X because that visit was actually compensation worth $X." Zoomers will look at their mobile bank, Robinhood, and Venmo accounts at the end of each month to get a feel for how much money they have. Shifting all the noncash benefits to cash benefits in a more straightforward salaried system would closely match civilian jobs and prevent shielding. Sure, the barracks would then charge rent like any other living arrangement, and healthcare would be deducted from your paycheck as used, but Zoomers could finally make an apples-to-apples comparison. The ease of comparison will enable a Zoomer to see that the military pays on par with civilian jobs or, if less, just how little less. Ultimately, this makes the joining decision much more quantifiable.

I remember in middle school when each of us would count our lunch money. We were all very careful to budget just enough to get a soft and doughy chocolate chip cookie on Fridays. The unchanging cafeteria prices and the fact that most of us got the same thing for lunch every day gave us the stability needed to make this calculation. I learned then from my young friends just how much humans crave stability and predictability, especially when it comes to pricing. Military pay currently doesn't allow for either because of the strange allowance-based system that it promotes.

Another reason to detour into pay discussions is to shield against the dangers of just throwing money at the military manpower problem. The reforms must be tempered not to tip the scales too far to promote profit. If we turn the paradigm around and say that we don't have enough money to fund a big all-volunteer standing army, so instead, we'd rather pay a smaller army with better skills, much more money, we begin to create a force that no longer serves the people. Currently, Russia is employing a highly specialized mercenary group to do some of its specialized fighting in Ukraine. This Wagner group is funded by a Russian oligarch and will answer to the wishes of the elites paying them rather than the citizenry. As warfare became highly specialized, the US has also employed private military contractors to carry out highly technical, highly skilled missions. Mercenaries have existed throughout history, and pay for modern soldiers of fortune is categorically higher than comparable government military pay.

Suppose society one day gives up on solving the recruiting crises and instead uses straight pay increases as its main lever for manpower. In that case, we'll create a more elite force that is better at specialized missions but smaller in number and less capable of defending the homeland it represents. This problem is addressed indirectly in the excellent book: *AWOL: The Unexcused Absence of America's Upper Classes from Military Service and How it Hurts Our Country* by Frank Schaeffer and Kathy Roth-Douquet.[67] On pages 133-134, they write, "Under this construct, military duty is compelling only if you personally choose the cause at hand or if it will in some way help your personal growth or your self-esteem. The idea of society choosing the cause, that you don't in fact even know what mission you might perform when you commit to serve, has become anathema to virtue-since no virtue (today in our modern culture) is possible without individual choice...At the same time that personal preference has come to reign supreme, the country has become more prosperous. Prosperity, for many people, has stimulated a reflex against things that are difficult, as if the goal of both childhood and adulthood is to avoid discomfort and risk. This development also works against the appeal of military service."

Following that, the upper class is currently significantly underrepresented in our military. Those with wealth are not currently influentially controlling one of America's strongest assets. While I agree with Roth-Douquet and Schaeffer that more upper-class Americans should be serving our nation, turning the military into such a compelling wealth generator like a mercenary army will attract the wrong people and be subject to bad influences. In essence, the military needs to continue to pull most of its recruits from the middle class and enable them to at least remain at that socioeconomic level and grow modestly over time. The last thing we want is a special operations military that sheds its core constituency: the average American with average skills and ability attempting to do the above-average thing out of the desire to serve.

The recruiting cycle should be detached from economic influences via side hustles and similar-job comparisons. However, part of that detachment includes keeping the force in check to answer to the people and the call for service, rather than the influence of just the dollar. We should enable troops to make more money and understand the actual value of what they're paid, but we shouldn't go so far as to make military service a path to getting rich for a select few.

Related to changing the way we present military work is what liberties we give those in uniform. Remote and mobile work are two new phenomena that are catching momentum with Generation Z. We'll now analyze how the military can incorporate this to create a more fulfilling workplace.

CHAPTER 10:

Allowing Changing Work Patterns In The Military

Some of the greatest military conquests of all time have been accomplished by nomadic warriors. Genghis Khan led the Mongols on horseback throughout Asia, and Alexander the Great streamed down from Greece to present-day India. Occasionally moving from one's home is deeply rooted in our hunter-gatherer genetics. As the world industrialized, travel receded, and everything humans needed to survive was closely located with them. While the urge to travel and explore is nothing new, Gen Z has more flexibility in both where they geographically want to work and when they choose to do so. The movement to remote work saw Z become the first generation to do the better portion of a year of online schooling. Zooming became the method of collaborating as purely digital meetings flourished. While the jury is out on whether permanent remote work is here to stay or not, the experience forged a generation that will continue to want to use innovation to increase optionality around location and distance. Z wants to have the flexibility of being remote combined with the experience of occasionally being mobile when crafting work for themselves in the 21st century.

Remote work to Z simply means work that is not done in person in their usual office place. Right off the bat, this concept rubs against what the traditional military is all about. Our military fights battles primarily in the physical domain, and nearly all training exercises are done in person. However, when COVID struck, the DoD scrambled like all organizations to get as many people as possible remotely connected to its networks to keep up productivity. Through the use of digital devices, the office was brought to the home in what first appeared to be a massive gain of freedom for workers. However, an MIT study classified what is now known as the autonomy paradox. What this is saying is that for those who were able to work anywhere all the time, then why ever stop working? Many ended up stretching out the work or school day, intermixing leisure activities with professional ones, and extending the hours of being "on" from morning right through bedtime. Remote work isn't necessarily more liberating or better. It just gives another dimension of flexibility. The critical insight that many Zers had was that they didn't need to be fully in-person nor fully remote. Z primarily liked the variability of having both, and this newfound flex schedule let them shape their lives as they wanted.

I'll never forget the strange comments many of my elders made when I entered the private civilian workforce during COVID. They remarked how I'll never meet my boss or I'll miss out on the mentorship conversations that happen in passing in an office. When I started, we had just moved into one of the nicest offices in D.C. complete with daily meal catering and views of the city. While many of the things my elders told me may hold true, and I am lucky to have eventually experienced a good amount of in-person work, there was a certain appeal to starting remotely and not being the fearful newbie in the office place. The flexibility of having the option was certainly a bonus.

This location/distance liberation is part of a much broader change where workers are reshaping traditional tasking. The reason remote work is even possible nowadays is that the nature of tasks is different now. Even for the military, which still requires human hands to physically pull gun triggers, most tasks are actually in the knowledge realm. The planning and administration, organizational briefing, and intelligence discovery that accompanies our work has shifted to digital computers and inside our collective cloud servers. The insightful "All-in" podcast, one of the top trending talk shows about tech, politics, and economics, discusses the concept of the narrator economy in Episode 111.[68] One of the commentators explains how in the economy as a whole, we've seen the transition from laborers to knowledge workers in the 1900s. In the 21st century, many creators, or those with thought leadership and idea entrepreneurship, have risen.

They posit that with powerful tools like artificial intelligence, we'll enter this new narrator economy shortly. In this new chapter of work, A.I. tools will even do much of the creating and thinking, while humans will have to be trained and rewarded for the best narration/interaction with the tools. Authors will no longer write books. The best ones will understand how to lay out their thoughts to an A.I. bot scribe. Military commanders will no longer write orders. Instead, the most successful ones will voice their goals and end state in a way that allows algorithms

WE DON'T WANT YOU, UNCLE SAM

to produce the best battle plans. While we may still be far off from seeing this realized–and in the meantime, there will be plenty of good young Americans required to turn wrenches for the DoD–this will soon trickle down to impact everyone's working style. This change of tasks that need to be done promotes the ability to break geographic bounds and allows even military members the flexibility to do occasional remote work when required/desired.

Coupled with but distinct from the concept of remote work is the desire in many Zers to experience mobile work. Mobile work is specifically work done while traveling. Mobile work isn't often about typing at random Starbucks, but rather traveling to farther states and even countries while still creating. While some aspects of Z make them more sedentary and stationary, the ability to connect with other young Zers from other countries has ignited a desire to occasionally travel around the world. Popular travel blogs and vlogs bring images and videos from across the earth to one's desktop. This has given rise to the now famous "digital nomad" movement, where many Zers are working from all over the globe while simultaneously bouncing around from place to place. The offer to travel and the appeal of seeing new places has always been a selling point to new recruits interested in a life of service. At the same time, constantly moving around is very unsettling when trying to start a family and lay down consistency. When discussing how parents can help raise their kids, an HBR professor writes, "A stable community and network of local friends and relationships can help kids develop strong roots. In turn, your global perspective as a corporate nomad can help you expand your children's vision."[69].

The trope of being a "military brat" that has to move locations every four years when your duty station changes is not appealing to prospective Z joiners. While the military is working hard to enable "homesteading" and reducing the number of moves certain families have to make, it must also continue to offer short-term maneuverability where trips and mobile work take place. So essentially, improving leave policies is the best way the military can balance keeping people in one place while simultaneously fulfilling Z's desire for occasional mobility. Currently, leave is very structured when on active duty, often restricting when you can travel and how far you can go. Requiring distance limitations and burdensome approval processes are not conducive to Gen Z. The number of automobiles and airline routes present today has essentially shrunk the entire continental U.S. into one easily accessible mega-city. Zers should be allowed to fly from base to their hometown on any weekend to see parents or even a friend.

Additionally, more airlines and corporations should be encouraged to sponsor troop flights on the holidays to support this mobility. The Armed Forces YMCA launched Operation Ride Home, which brought 2,000 junior enlisted service members home for Thanksgiving and Christmas. This represents the ultimate effectiveness of a public-private partnership where patriotic citizens can directly impact young Zers. Showing that a mobile lifestyle is possible even after joining the military and getting stationed somewhere supports the recruiting effort.

The military needs to work to incorporate the best of remote work and occasionally mobile lifestyles to enable Z to move forward. This newfound flexibility enabled by innovation is essentially a demand by Z for employers to harness tech benefits while increasing the overall work experience. Allowing military members to Zoom into specific meetings or incorporating a more agile schedule for tasks that don't need physical presence will be a step in the right direction. What this expansion of location and distance has meant when it comes to new working patterns is essentially that disaggregated teams can harness modern tools to remain just as impactful. Going back to the nomadic warriors, while they covered great distances, their armies were still confined by spatial limitations for command and control. Communication was slow, so the entire Army had to travel by giant caravan so that messages could be passed to all troops. We progressed to the radio and telephone in the 1900s, but now with smartphones and tablets, we're able to essentially be in the same mental room as someone even when thousands of miles separate our bodies. This trend will only accelerate, and the organizations that promote it best will win the war for talent.

Increasing remote work and encouraging more lax leave policies for Zers are the two talked about recommendations that enable this remote/mobile perception shift. On a more fundamental level, the mindset change that comes with modernizing strict ways of doing things will be the biggest impediment to seeing some of this enacted. Any forward-leaning leader who comes out and announces that certain members of the unit can do some tasks remotely is going to inevitably get hit with flak from troops used to "the old way." These gradual and long-term institutional evolutions will not simply boost recruiting overnight. Instead, the knowledge that "hey, the military allows me to do some remote work" will have to slowly seep out into the general psyche of Z. Perhaps the best way to shed light on this new military life is to serialize what so many military Zers are already promoting on their Youtube/Tik-Tok/Instagram channels.

Military Zers making videos are already capturing the essence of new service life every day, just in a distributed way. While many other occupations, from home decoration on HGTV to police work on the former show *Cops*, have showcased those professions' day-to-day, the military hasn't formally done this yet. Mike Rowe may have featured the military on "Dirty Jobs," but the fact that thousands of movies and t.v. dramas have been made about the military without one real break-through reality show is puzzling.

To truly market this organizational change that is underway with remote/mobile opportunities, the military should invest in making a reality Netflix series about everyday military life. It wouldn't have to be flashy, and the public affairs personnel are more than capable of producing the series that would hit Z in a medium they are familiar with. It wouldn't be one focused on grueling special forces training or daring missions but would simply document the day-to-day work life of junior enlisted Zers as they describe what they do. Currently tons of Youtube personalities interview military members about their daily life. Some of these have more satirical takes, but the content is being generated and is certainly available for viewing. It would be interesting to gather data on how many young Z recruits corroborate what their recruiters tell them by searching something in the Youtube/Instagram shorts database. The point is, the military again needs to lean forward on a trend already happening and demonstrate the new life experience that Zers in uniform are getting. Through initiatives like this, the impact of new organizational changes like remote and mobile work will finally be understood by the recruiting pool.

Remote, mobile, or in-person, the actual work military members are doing is also rapidly changing. New training and reskilling have to be continuous in order to keep up. We'll now examine how the military itself can be used as a great reskilling tool for its employees.

CHAPTER 11:
Reskilling the Labor Force Through Military Jobs

There's the often-repeated expression that 40 is the new 30. For Z, a better trope would be that 30 is the new 20, since you can become a better version of your past self. With further research and investment in anti-aging lifestyles,[70][71] science is delivering the first generation to live forever (or, more realistically, the first generation in modern times to achieve a massive 5-10 year jump in life expectancy). While the military has traditionally recruited from a young age pool, the most significant opportunity to attract Z may still be years away. As the oldest Zers turn 26, it's reasonable to prepare to continue to make the military appeal to them for at least a decade and a half more. As Zoomers continue to age, there are positive reasons to believe that their grit and ability to get challenging jobs done will increase over time.[72]Counteracting this positive trajectory will be that the skills needed to stay current in a dynamic world economy will be ever-changing. Future Zers at later ages in life are a recruiting pool that will need skills to remain relevant. The military can offer the reskilling program that Zers are looking for.

An older gen Z group may be an extremely fruitful recruiting pool. Z is now at the peak of what has traditionally been the most important troop age. However, as generations age out, the military often lets them go in favor of the younger generation that follows. For this time, focusing on Gen Z as a whole and adapting and following them well past their first jobs and into their second "adult" decade may be the winning strategy. Predicting future outcomes based on data and statistics has never been easy. Wall Street spends billions each year trying to gain some inside edge on the terabytes of available data, and the military, with much less cash, has to do the same predictive analytics. The DoD may not be continually nimble enough to adjust itself each generation that goes by. By the time Generation Alpha is ready to be the primary recruiting thrust, there won't be enough time for the military to reinvent itself again. Instead, the military should "go long" and bet on Z with the hopes of recruiting them over more age periods. To again borrow from investing, the play here uses time arbitrage.

By adapting to Z now while planning to appeal to them for the long haul, the DoD can generate recurring returns because Z is already a generation that has been shown to mature later in various aspects of life. This later maturity after a period of self-exploration may drive some Zers who initially reneged on the recruiting pitch to have second thoughts when they inevitably go through one of their initial career switches. Instead of staying true to the typical 18-24 bubble, expanding that bubble can be the key to success. While history is littered with sensational stories about how the young often rise against an impending enemy to save the old, the "Graybeards" of the Civil War uniquely stand out. This Iowa unit consisted of 45-year-old+ volunteers who helped the Union guard prisoners and even saw combat action. There is indeed a past precedent of Americans joining at a much older age to defend the nation. Taking a look at wars fought in the rest of the world and that precedent is even more common.

The most appealing part of an older Z population relates to educational trends. One of the four major disqualifiers the DoD has mentioned relates to educational standing. Many Americans today, who either didn't graduate high school or obtain a satisfactory score on the armed forces entry exam, are deemed unfit for service. Occasionally, an educational waiver may be granted, but the policy is missing out on a paradigm shift regarding skills acquisitions in the modern economy. Firstly, many jobs today are task-based and iterative. They are constantly innovating, and it matters more about if you can learn and adapt rather than what you know because of what a piece of paper with your name on it says. If we flip this on its head and assume that Z thinks more pragmatically than their parents, many will quickly realize that a degree is not the answer. Then the logical conclusion is that Z cares most about skills attainment to do what is asked of them in the economy. Many Zers realize that jobs are updating so fast that in just a few years, a previously qualified candidate will need to be retrained on the latest methods, practices, or tools. This is especially true for technical, computer-related jobs but is also increasingly common in the trades sector. Our human hardware (our brain and DNA) is not adapting fast enough to our societal software (our innovative new knowledge and tools for productivity).

On the opposite end of highly academic degrees come technical and trades degree programs. These courses (sometimes apprenticeships) emphasize hands-on work and on-the-job training. The common knowledge that plumbers make excellent money is also beginning to hold true for many other trade jobs due to their increasingly high demand. If college is no longer a mandatory need for everyone and it's reasonable to say that core/essential ability can be obtained through technical/online/apprentice-like programs,[73] then DoD policy change is needed. Drawing a hard line in the sand and rejecting those without a high school degree or unable to pass a military entrance test is harmful to current and future Gen Z recruitment. The kid who dropped out of high school to work as a mechanic and has been doing so for ten years perhaps brings a much greater capability to the operating forces than an 18-year-old who passed science class. With nearly ~95-98% of servicemembers having a high-school degree already, increasing recruiting numbers and bringing in more without a high school degree but with skills and perhaps the ability to be trained for the qualifying test, will not weaken the force or reduce standards. Even a 5-10% drop in high school graduates would likely keep performance high while significantly impacting recruiting.

The most profound way that the military can capitalize on this need for later-in-life skills is to become the best reskilling program in the world. Allowing more educational waivers is one recommendation for those without a high school degree, but becoming the very organization that fills the training gap for outdated workers is the master stroke. What is already happening but will reach an actual tipping point in the next decade as Zers pass through their twenties is the re-learning phenomenon. Those who are usually rebounding from their earliest experiences and coming back for round two jobs will be a massive group needing to up their talent in a few years. Whole cohorts of workers will have to get "re-educated, reskilled, and upskilled"[74] to keep up with machines, A.I., and the roaring exponential pace of economic advancement.[75]

Upskilling is when workers are taught new skills within their current job to make them more productive. Think of a racecar getting a better engine to go faster. Reskilling is when employees learn new skills for a new job that may be totally different. Think of a racecar that is now putting on a ball hitch to haul trailers around. While the exact path a future Zer goes down may differ, the track doesn't have to include someone going back to formal schooling for an advanced degree or looking to the private sector. The single best return on investment an organization can make is one in training its employees. From a national perspective, the best thing our military can do to make better and more productive citizens is to continually train them and provide them with skills. Suppose it can successfully become that the military is the best retraining experience for mid-career Zers. In that case, an economic and manning problem will be solved simultaneously. The infrastructure already exists for this seismic shift to take place.

In the past, the military has been credited with being the engine behind American prosperity and innovation. From DARPA's creation of the internet to the fact that the G.I. Bill after WWII created billions in GDP value, America has formerly relied on its military to propel it into more prosperous times. Both my grandfathers benefitted from the military supporting their education as young men, but I am still wonderstruck when thinking that neither of them learned how to turn on a computer in their 90+ years of life. Had either of them somehow ventured back into military service in their later years, they literally wouldn't be able to function without basic typing skills. The main point here is that while the military is often very risk-averse and its bureaucracy is extremely slow to adapt to changes (one of the reasons this book exists), it will still move faster than a good portion of many citizens' jobs. Believe it or not, there are millions of Americans that are employed in areas of the economy that move even slower than the military. This won't include fast-moving biotechs or extremely well-run small businesses, but there are plenty of Mom and Pop shops that exist for decades with relatively little skill investment or the need to change. For this group, having a fall-back program that teaches practical skills is an absolute must if those companies are ever to close or those people one day desire to change careers.

Military schools are already as practical as they can be…often cramming an abundance of learning into too short of a time. The military must harness digital education to lure reskillers in and truly land this trend. By using civilian online platforms like Udemy, Coursera, and Pluralsight, the military can offer civilians reskilling courses even before they join. A job like supply or logistics, which are crucial functions in the military, now so closely matches the civilian sector that there is no need to hoard all the DoD knowledge in in-person schoolhouses. Making MOOCS (massive open online courses) available to civilians where all the case studies and readings revolve around military matters would enable civilians to acquire skills like military service members. Some of these re/upskillers may then look to join the service, but even those that don't will come away with better qualifications. The initiative would also save DoD time so that they wouldn't have as long wait queues for class-ups, and those with completed course credits before joining can move quickly into a unit after basic training.

The overarching movement would see a lot of unclassified knowledge that is often taught in a death-by-PowerPoint manner in the schoolhouse moved online to allow fellow citizens to learn new ideas and skills. Firstly, the military as a whole would do a lot better to move many of its briefs and decision meetings off of powerpoint slides with pretty colors and into written narrative format. Amazon does this expertly well because it recognizes that written thought papers are much better for coming to consensus and disseminating knowledge than powerpoints. Nonetheless, I digress to explain that the military can and should simply share these powerpoints to larger audiences. The content is already created, and the exposure these civilians would get to military problem sets may spark a latent interest in actual service. The military itself is already working on supporting troops who do distance education externally, so non-affiliated civilians should be included in this. The number of YouTube videos and tutorials about how to grow skills that would flow from DoD knowledge would be astounding. It might even be worth considering offering a tax credit to incentivize citizens to up their skills. Almost like a reverse G.I. bill where currently Veterans get money to go back to school after service, here citizens would get incentivized to re-learn from the military after school.

By educating themselves in particularly military matters/approaches to common functional trades like supply, logistics, and maintenance, Americans will be increasing their productivity. Even leadership courses are an option. Society seems to love military leadership books and stories to the point that making unclassified DoD leadership lectures and schooling available would likely be a massive hit. There is a wall of untapped knowledge currently hiding behind the military-civilian divide. Letting that flow outward would bring significant gains to the entire population.

Lastly, the purpose of learning and getting training is to gain non-in-tuitive, tacit knowledge. Explicit knowledge like facts and stories can be read alone (a teacher may be needed to tell you what to read, but even without guidance, someone can get by). A welding manual is an example of explicit knowledge. The fundamental goal of all repetitions and practice in higher education, trade schools, and apprenticeships is to gain tacit knowledge. A welder who looks at a hinge and knows precisely how to fix it relies on tacit knowledge. Tacit knowledge is achieved through life experience, often by being surrounded by mentors who can help fine-tune your dataset. Tacit knowledge is when your intuition is primed so you "just know."

You think and feel the answer even before it comes to your head. Some specific members of Z will have already built this essential tacit knowledge by the time they are ready to join the military later in life. This older cohort will have accumulated niche skill sets that can augment what the DoD currently has and teaches. Some more senior members may be uniquely qualified to enter at higher ranks/pay grades if they have this corresponding civilian sector experience. While such initiatives initially cause a stir among the traditionalists, making a highly qualified technical expert go to basic boot camp at age 30 will steer those phenotypes away. Instead, there should be increased lateral-entry expert contracts to get more of them in uniform.

Z is a generation that will mature and grow grittier over time. As they age, their mindset to achieve whatever task is at hand will increase. Challenging these developing abilities will be the fact that jobs will get increasingly more complex and need possible reskilling/upskilling intervention to keep Zers relevant in the workforce. This presents a massive opportunity for the military to continue to recruit later-in-life Zers who need new skill sets. If the DoD allows itself to be the best re-trainer of the generation, it will yield incredible recruiting rewards.

As Part 2 concludes and the midway point of the book is reached, I wanted to mention the type of change discussed so far. "Modernizing" the military workplace to make it in line with Gen Z expectations is certainly not easy. It is absolutely going to require the right people in Congress, the DoD, and the armed forces to create momentum. After all, solving these "people" issues comes down to well, people, with the willpower to do something. It should be noted though that most of these recommendations so far are internal facing, and can indeed be altered by those in power. In part 3, we'll look at larger societal influences that are more out of our control, but the aforementioned is in our direct control. They are policies within our institution that are amendable. Even though the military is gigantic, it's not impervious to original thinking and motivated groups who want to see improvement.

The essential ingredient is continued exposure to these ideas. Professor Adam Grant in his book *Originals* writes, "Overall, the evidence suggests that liking continues to increase as people are exposed to an idea between ten and twenty times, with additional exposure still useful for more complex ideas."[76] This may seem logical, but in reality it's anathema to how things are done currently. Every year Congress has one or two hearings where they grill experts on how to make the military more appealing to recruits. Then perhaps there are one or two big General conferences within DoD policyland to discuss changes. Maybe a few working groups or reports get published, but very little substantive change goes on, at least not on the order of magnitude that's needed. Recruiting should be top of mind of every single person who touches the DoD, from entry-level privates to the most distant civilian contractors working in chow halls. These discussions need to be happening every day to the point where small unit leaders can actually echo up the chain of command these internal cultural changes that would make our organization better. This is a direct call to the reader to spread these ideas, your own, or anyone else's about DoD recruitment to as many people as possible.

Viewing Aspects of Larger Society That Impact Gen Z Military Recruitment

During the 2016 election, I was a freshman in my first semester of college. My age cohort was the only Gen Zers who were able to vote, but all Zoomers will remember the divisiveness of that period. We learned in school that elections were supposed to be exciting and fun, but now the country appeared to be splitting in half before our eyes. Democrats and Republicans seemed to hate each other and in some places stopped talking altogether. I was puzzled by the intensity of everyone's reaction. Parents stopped talking to children on the opposing side, violent protests broke out, and consistently my elders reminded me that "they've never seen anything like this." For a generation that was just given the exciting right to vote, it seemed like we did wrong just by taking part in the process. As time dulls those memories, all of us will go to the ballot boxes and still recall something from that vitriolic time. From that moment on, politics seemed more like a brutal necessity rather than an exciting expression of democracy.

In Part 3, I discuss the various social and cultural factors in modern America that affect Generation Z. Many will find these to be the most opinionated and controversial chapters, but arguably the most important ones. From politics to drugs to mental health, many of today's hot-button issues are discussed in relation to how they are impacting the military's recruitment efforts.

CHAPTER 12:

Unplugging from an Always-On World

Generation Z is known as the first true digital natives. That trendy nickname implies that its members were born online. To say that Z exists primarily in the screen world and then only secondarily in the physical world is wrong. There is no doubting the huge impact that technology has had on Zoomers. However, a deeper counter-trend is also emerging below the surface of all these screens, one of unplugging. Since Z innately understands the power of technology and its use in everyday life better than any previous generation, they also fundamentally grasp its ability to infiltrate basic humanity. On a first principles level, Z realizes that too much of a good thing is a bad thing. Z is acutely aware of the negative impacts of overusing, and many members even attempt (some unsuccessfully) self-regulation.[77] Having the willpower to make that desired habit change is hard, and Z will probably need the support of the greater society. Z is reaching out for real-world connections as they recognize the problems of becoming too absorbed in the digital world. Constant pinging and always being on a device is crushing Gen Z. The generation is reported to be more depressed and more suicidal than any other group in modern history. They are beginning to crave some time unplugged to reset. This is evidenced by the numerous Z-centric support groups that seek to end technology addiction. The military can offer this real-world, responsibility-bearing, unplugged experience that many seek.

Video games offer the perfect counterintuitive example to highlight how Z wants to collect experiences in the real world. When the first Nintendo games came out, they were undoubtedly revolutionary and exciting, but like any laboratory-made drug, they had their limits. Now, video games have evolved into dopaminergic nirvana that floods the brain with its most potent experience-seeking chemical. Quick update speeds and novel game maps are scientifically manufactured to give users an overloading, addictive high. Popular neuroscience podcaster Andrew Huberman remarks that "some studies show video games release Dopamine on a level between that of nicotine and cocaine.[78]" More and more Zers are getting into gaming, and an entire culture is cropping up around it. However, it's important to examine what types of games teens play nowadays. Action-adventure and role-playing/storyline games take a significant share of the market. While it's true that the basic competitive and shooter/racer genres exist with big followings, these other gaming groups hint at a possible deeper insight. When the world closed during lockdowns, many isolated Zers retreated into their consoles for a sense of the traditional human explorative journey.

This yearning to explore and venture out is more than typical teenage rebelliousness. Any review of movies from any decade in the 1900s will hint at this same "getting away from society and finding yourself" trend. That isn't what is going on here with Z. It's not about getting away to explore some deeper unknown or see someplace (any Zer can look that up in two seconds on Google). Instead, it's about collecting experiences, just like a video game character collects objectives on a quest. One big takeaway Z had from COVID was that specific experiences couldn't wait because they are no longer guaranteed. That family wedding, high school graduation, quinceanera, sweet 16 that was always supposed to happen was either postponed or canceled. So Z retreated to very addicting worlds where they could create their own experiences. The constant push to make these products more life-like and realistic is a weak substitute for real-world adventures. Meta's massive investment most recently evidences this malaise for the newer and shinier games in virtual reality. Surprisingly, "half of the 7,100 teens surveyed in financial firm Piper Sandler's biannual Gen Z research project said they were unsure or had zero intention of purchasing a device to access the metaverse[79]".

Induced even before the virus, the undercurrent of Z's desire for experiences stems from the larger American economy's shift from manufacturing and products to services. Today more than 80% of employed Americans work in service-related jobs, as opposed to 1959 when the number was closer to 50%. Furthermore, over 109 million jobs exist in the services sectors, while the goods sector peaked at 25 million in 1979 and has been stagnant since.[80] As this movement away from goods has accelerated, Gen Z has followed suit in becoming less materialistic and more experiential. Z doesn't desire the consumption of goods, but rather the consumption of experiences and the creation of memories. Z would rather go to an escape room than watch a movie, they'd instead do a bar crawl than buy a craft beer, and they'd rather see an event than receive a present. *Harvard Business Review* published an article titled "Welcome to the Experience Economy."[81] The thesis of the paper argued that we're chasing experiences more than ever in a world where most lands have already been discovered. Z is fully aware that only in the real world can specific experiences happen. Although the addictive power of the virtual world is blinding and causes many Zers to be sucked too far in, the generation knows in their hearts that more meaningful experiences exist in the physical realm. The issue now for Z is how to break away from an increasingly intoxicating digital sphere, how to take the avatars they create in fantasyland and become them in reality land.

Related to avatars and fantasies, pornography is a significant area where Gen Z recognizes the crushing effects of computers. Online porn sites have exploded in popularity in the past decade with an exponentially increasing number of videos and varieties of categories. While many millennials were frequent viewers of free, online porn made by professionally paid actors, a relatively recent trend witnessed by generation Z has been the emergence of Onlyfans.com. Onlyfans[82] is a growing site where consumers directly interact with and pay amateur content creators who oftentimes engage in sexual acts. With more than 170 million subscribers and tons of new ones signing up daily, the platform is expected to grow enormously. Regardless of whether porn is being accessed for free or in a more curated, paid format, the impact internet porn is having on Generation Z is massive.[83]

To start, increased viewing of visual internet porn is often medically associated with issues such as loneliness[84], anxiety, and sexual impotence. What's more, just like video games, porn content has become more abundant and addictive. As an aside, the group suffering most (both in numbers and severity) from this addiction is young, heterosexual males.

This cohort struggling with the epidemic[85] of porn addiction relates to the military as an institution, with its members being over 80% male.[86] The real implication, however, is not Z's usage of porn but rather its newer outlook on watching pornography. Although many, likely even the majority of, members of Z are still watching porn, they are beginning to realize its negative effects and are trying to end addictive use. The #NoFap movement is one such growing collective that is trying to encourage a reduction in porn usage. While only currently existing in a disaggregated online counterculture, NoFap is growing and Zers are increasingly talking about their battles with reducing addiction. Z's active effort to deal with this further demonstrates their increased desire to "unplug" from another part of their lives that negatively impacts them.

NoFap is still just a thought. Collecting statistical data on any emerging trend is problematic due to the multiplatform way that Z interacts online. What's important to note is that sometimes these online anonymous discussion groups where ideas like NoFap originate can have enormous effects on the psyche of the entire Z generation. Many will recall the hysteria in early 2021 with the meme stock movement. A phenomenon that started as a Reddit group called Wallstreetbets took the world by storm as it saw that retail investors from the internet could take on the financial titans of Wall Street as they battled for control of GameStop. Overall, analyzing tucked-away parts of the chat rooms yield revealing clues to understand what Gen Z is thinking and how they behave. Various studies also show a generation that is participating less in drinking and sexual activity.[87]

This has even prompted some to tag Z as the "puriteens." Another trend creeping up in the recesses of the internet has been known as "mil-toks." These tik-toks are geared explicitly towards a military audience, and often show videos of uniformed service members participating in their daily jobs and making memes or cultural commentaries. Most of these are harmless inside jokes that only current military members would understand. Some are actually (whether intentionally or unintentionally) motivating videos that subconsciously serve as recruiting reinforcements. Still others, are probably the most candid and realistic depictions of day-to-day life in the military.

One category of these "mil-toks" related to the discussion of porn, and Gen Z's realization that some tech trends are not positive relates to "thirst traps." Thirst traps are videos that, according to the Urban Dictionary, are made "for the intent of causing others to publicly profess their attraction. This is done not to actually respond or satisfy any of this attraction, but to feed the poster's ego or need for attention."[88] While thirst traps represent only a small subgenre of the "mil-toks," there has been increasing chatter online about the use of attractive people in uniform to entice military-aged potential recruits to join the armed services.

From pretty faces on World War Two recruiting posters to honeypot techniques used in cold war spying, sex and the military have a storied past. Z, however, is uniquely aware of how this is unhealthy and wishes to avoid being influenced. One recent incident highlighting this has been the explosion of followers for one tik-toker who goes by "Lunchbag Lujan." The army soldier Hailey Lujan appears to be a psychological operations specialist and has gained millions of followers. This is many more than almost all military recruiting accounts. The fact that she is openly a member of a psychological operations unit has thrown the Z webchats into a tizzy, wondering if this person (who many deem to be attractive) is an actual psychological operation funded by the U.S. government to induce recruitment. The greater conversation again points out Z's skepticism of the internet, and recognition that various parts of their beloved social media may be manipulative when consumed in large doses.

After identifying the trend that Z realizes some of the adverse effects of technology, the question becomes how the military can successfully convert that to boost recruitment. Video game usage shows a desire for real-world experiences, and attempts to curtail porn addictions highlight increased responsibility drives. Many Zers are self-imposing screen time limits in general. Fully taking technology out of the equation for a certain period of time could meet this generation's desires. The military can offer this real-world, responsibility-bearing, limited technology experience with the most effective screentime reset around. In boot camp, nearly no phones or technology allow new recruits to defeat the negative impact of the tech they've come to need. However, simply talking about the benefits of "unplugging" and going to an experience like boot camp isn't going to do much to help the military's case. More tangible actions need to occur in tandem.

One Marine Corps recruiter tapped into recent anime obsessions and redrew old-style Marine recruiting posters with new designs.[89] This outside-the-box thinking helps to show how the military is the real-world journey many video games attempt to deliver. The Army has started these great 15-second snappy videos as part of their "know your Army" campaign displaying the many health, financial, and career benefits the Army offers. However, they should go one step further and make one showing how military life can be the much-desired reprieve from the stresses of everyday online society. There's even a term for malaise among Z called "tech-fatigue." Numerous blogs have proliferated amongst our generation as self-improving individuals proclaim how powering down has greatly impacted their lives. Some are beginning to recognize the benefits of taking breaks from being constantly plugged in, but many don't know exactly where to turn to awaken from the matrix that has become an "always-on" life.

Every summer in the Adirondacks, a unique, almost ritualistic tradition plays out for many young Americans. Sleepaway camp brings together hundreds of children from various states (mostly the Northeast, Florida, and California) for seven weeks of nonstop activity and personal growth in isolated mountains. Some of my best friends came from that time because we were isolated from the world and undistracted, we could form stronger bonds. Trying to describe camp to someone unfamiliar with it is like describing the United States Marine Corps' Officer Candidates' School. In both situations, you sleep in a large open room (a squad bay vs. a bunk), you eat three meals a day in a massive hall (a chow hall vs. a dining hall), and you have older adults chaperone you around to various activities (sergeant instructors vs. counselors). The only difference is the goal and end state. At OCS, the objective is to make the experience as humanly stressful as possible. Ideally to push a person to their limits, and determine if they have the necessary leadership attributes to become an Officer in the Marine Corps. At sleepaway camp, the goal is to make each day as humanly blissful as possible. Ideally to cater to each camper's dreams, and ultimately create memories and friendships that shape the development of that child. Still, one key detail also stands out: both places confiscate all phones and electronics at the beginning, allowing for a nearly technology-free experience with no internet.

To truly drive home the point of disconnecting from the dangers Z sees with technology, the military should try to partner with local towns near bases to encourage the reduction of technology usage for one hour a month at a specific agreed-upon time. While weekly breaks from tech have been enormously beneficial to practitioners of a "tech sabbath," those choices lie with individuals. Instead, collective towns can experiment with small acts of unplugging and joining in with bases to see how their youth recognize the gains from not succumbing to the negatives Z has already identified with tech. As time went on, that hour could extend to a few or even a whole day once a year, like the National Day of Unplugging[90] supports. The cultural exercise of doing this would move American society closer to seeing how an unplugged life at the beginning of military training is beneficial. Joining the military isn't an act... instead, it is a place you go, an experience toward a destination. That destination is one where being unplugged is sometimes worth everything it took to get there.

Every Zer today remembers the first time they became "plugged-in.". It may have been scrolling on their parents' phone, getting their first video game, or simply typing on a computer for the first time. This moment of connecting to the online world set a path for us at a young age of digital literacy. The tech-craving habits we developed as youngsters have stuck with many of us since. Next we'll discuss the habit of physical self-defense that has seemingly retreated in modern society. In order to create the next warrior class, this is something we should explore bringing back.

CHAPTER 13:

Creating Future Warriors at a Young Age

Physical violence has been and will always be part of warfare. It's uncomfortable and challenging to discuss, but warfare requires killing other human beings. Militaries have long struggled with making their Soldiers physically strong enough to commit violence, and mentally sure enough to engage an enemy on the battlefield. If the war in Ukraine has shown the world anything, it's that even in modern times, extreme levels of destructive acts need to be done by warriors fighting for survival. Generation Z has grown up to primarily see physical violence as outdated and taboo. While cyberbullying rates and suicides have skyrocketed among Zers, old-style fisticuffs are not as common.

The Center for Disease Control's 2019 Youth Risk Behavior Survey reported that 8% of high school students had been in a physical fight one or more times in the past year[91]. In 1991, that number was nearly 50% among high schoolers. This decrease in physical violence has transferred over to the horrors of emotional and cyber violence; which some could argue are more damaging to our youth. Additionally, society must analyze the impact that the reduction of physical violence has on those it asks to go to war. Fighting is taboo in today's society, but making a representative warrior class will need to encourage some levels of teaching controlled physical violence in schools.

The specific distinction here is that "controlled is measured when it can be planned carefully. But oftentimes it is done in reaction to a crisis or bad event. It's measured in that those committing it aren't seeking to inflict any more damage than is necessary. The best corollary to this is using a taser (an act of controlled physical violence) to subdue an assailant with a knife. The distinction is also a physical one. Until we can alter each other's atoms in the digital world, biological organisms like humans will need to be physically impacted by other humans. Specifically, I prefer to use the term controlled physical violence rather than martial arts or self-defense. In a world that is now abundant with powerful natural language processing tools, we shouldn't mince words. There's nothing inherently "defensive" about a group of young servicemembers going on a raid to hunt and kill a terrorist.

This echoes some of the key teachings of training I've learned in the Marine Corps. Nate Fick, author of *One Bullet Away: The Making of a Marine Officer*[92] writes, "Marine training is essentially a battle against the instinct of self-preservation." One of the biggest wake-up calls for me was just how physically raw military training is. During my first interpersonal violence grappling match, a tough kid pinned me in thirty seconds, shoving my face into the ground and leaving me gasping for air. Better, more experienced, and much smarter authors like Fick have written much more on this topic, but my simple point is that we are training to commit violence unto other humans. A small subset will still have to be frontline combat arms. We will always need some subset of Americans to be able to do that and commit controlled physical violence.

The people fighting America's wars today come from an increasingly small subset of the population. When the draft existed back in WWII, nearly every member of America's "greatest generation" knew someone who served. Now, a specific warrior class has emerged in our professionalized, top-rate military. One New York Times article titled "…Makeup of U.S. Recruits Shows Growing Disparity[93]" perfectly summarizes the issue. "In 2019, 79% of Army recruits reported having a family member who served, and for nearly 30 percent, it was a parent – a striking point in a nation where less than 1 percent of the population serves in the military. Exposure to the military often comes primarily from familial connections nowadays, so it follows the logic that legacy military families dominate the force. Familiarity is now a stronger predictor of recruitment than race, class, or employment. In the popular action film, Jack Reacher, an Army veteran played by Tom Cruise, exclaims "There are four types of people who join the military. For some, it's a family trade. Others are patriots eager to serve. Next, you have those who need a job. Then there's the kind who want the legal means of killing other people."[94]

The family business part of that fictional line is beginning to ring true. As the proportion of military members comes from an increasingly smaller number of military families, we are beginning to lose the all-American fighting spirit that has sustained our forces throughout the past centuries. The divide between those serving and the rest of society is creating a widening gap that is dangerous for the health of an institution that is supposed to be governed by the people and for the people. Even the great writer of history Alexis de Tocqueville[95] remarked about the challenges a democratic nation like America will have when its military isn't representative of the country. A shrinking group is shouldering the violence, scars, and pain of war. Additionally, the mentality, skills, and will to wage wars are being upheld by this same small group. If this trend continues, America will cease to have a truly representative military but rather a small warrior class, like how the Japanese had samurai or the English and French had knights. If only the warrior class knows how to commit organized violence, then their power to one day rule over society through strength would become unchecked. While American society at large is no longer warlike, the skills of the warrior class, specifically the ability to commit physical violence, must be spread out to the entire population.

The specific violence that Generation Z has experienced in schools has been arguably the most deadly type in American history. Firstly, horrific school shootings have plagued the entirety of generation Z's childhood. It's the sad truth that Zoomers have become accustomed to monthly active shooter drills, and nearly every student daydreams about class escape plans. The mental impact is even worse. Z is the first generation where, since the 2012 Sandy Hook Elementary massacre, there has been at least one mass school shooting every 231 days.[96] Our schools have been turned into warlike battlegrounds. Teachers who have gone into the profession of educating children are being asked to sacrifice their lives in combat settings without any training or protective gear. It's baffling to some of us junior officers that more combat scenes will be seen in our hometowns than on our current deployments. The political right and left will continually argue about gun control vs. mental health reform. America will sadly lead the world in school shootings until a courageous group of politicians works together on complex, long-term solutions to alter the status quo. This can't even be classified as physical violence, but rather senseless violent slaughter when bullets are piercing notebooks and desks are being turned into last-resort bunkers.

Cyberbullying has also created more emotional violence for Zers. The ability to hide behind screens and stab with anonymous virtual knives leads to scars that cut deeper than any bodily wound. There was a Gen Z discussion on CNN on December 15, 2022, about office speak where older newscasters were learning from a Zoomer employee how to better talk to Z colleagues. She explained that ending sentences with periods seems too harsh, picking the wrong smile option can send bad signals, or how a thumbs up is passive aggressive similar to texting k as opposed to kk.[97] These little formalities set up by online chats and written text communications are small ways that Zers are harming each other mentally. We're losing the ability to talk naturally, which is creating distance between us. The level of suicide has never been higher for any American group of young people. From 2012 onward, there has been a statistically significant increase in youth suicides. Even just the 10-12-year-old group has seen a 5x jump from ingestion alone.[98] The adage of sticks and stones breaking bones while words never hurt is wholly debunked. Words don't just hurt; in the virtual world, they kill. Future warfighters are now facing an educational environment where they must fear getting shot or carefully navigate the minefield of online interactions without having their souls crushed.

Coupling the new violence Z has to face with its warriors coming from an increasingly small lineage leaves a majority of Zoomers hunting for modern rites of passage. With America's rapidly adapting society, it's sometimes easy to forget that all of us stem from more basic cultural roots. A study of history will show that most cultures had clearly defined rites of passage that marked key life milestones. While we still have amazing life events like baptisms, weddings, and graduations, our more primal welcoming into society has largely vanished. Looking at warrior societies from Europe, Asia, and Africa shows that nearly all future warriors underwent a culminating event demonstrating their physical ability to protect the larger tribe. The Maasai tribe of Kenya had lion hunts, while the ferocious Spartans of Greece had to kill Helot slaves. While both practices may seem abhorrent nowadays, the more significant point is that a physical act of courage and sacrifice was often deemed necessary to show society that you had the responsibility to become a contributing adult member.

Today, it's essential to note that Z is hungry for their rite of passage moments since they don't exist in a structured way anymore. Specific communities have versions, but none genuinely bind together the entire generation. Additionally, showing society one is worthy of responsibility rarely includes a physically violent act in the modern world, but in the ancient world, it almost always did. Many have lost touch with their ancestral roots and the way life cycles would occur for thousands of years. Today Zoomers are trying to codify the process of moving from child to adult, but they often don't have a good framework for when that transition occurs. They end up lost, many never properly making that key transition.

The country will always need people willing to commit physical violence in warfare to win our battles and successfully defend the nation. With mass drafts and the concept of a military that ramps up only when needed during wartime, the U.S. has embodied the citizen-soldier ethos first laid out by George Washington. Many comparisons were made between our first commander-in-chief and the legendary Roman general Cincinnatus, who temporarily took a hiatus from farming to protect his republic. That model of the citizen-soldier is a relic of history. With the new all-volunteer force, we have created a professionalized military deemed the toughest and most capable. We've moved away from all forms of physical displays of warriors and leave even those with the propensity to protect to act out their desires in online video games or imaginary-world chat rooms. The public school systems must begin training an actual warrior capability in physical education. Two positive externalities of this would be to get physical bodies into better shape and also to inculcate a stronger mindset. Aiding the fight against the obesity and mental health crises would be an excellent second-order effect.

Gym class has long been the ire of school administrators and state politicians. Some have argued that cutting it out of the curriculum will allow students to study more. Others have argued that letting kids be kids and blow off steam in the middle of the school day is hugely beneficial for health. Complicating this matter further is the fact that nearly every state and district has a different gym policy and its unique ways of structuring physical education.[99] Regardless of how it is currently structured, it would be a great boon to America's society if various forms of martial arts and self-defense (the practices that would lead to teaching the ability to commit controlled physical violence) were heavily emphasized in gym classes. With careful planning and supervision, programs that combine various forms of self-defense practices in a safe and protected manner would be effective. They can help teach this in all schools to make a more representative future warrior class. If more elements of society are exposed to the basics of interpersonal defense and offense, more will possess some critical fundamental skills that only specific subsets currently have.

Additionally, this activity will serve as a key outlet for aggression and solving disputes in a more hands-on manner rather than more damaging means. It's important to caveat that this isn't a call for fight clubs or brutal slugging to be going on during gym. It is a call for the way schools teach gym to be fundamentally reexamined, and an appeal that some form of physical defense and fighting technique is taught a few times a year to every age group. With the proper training, something local military professionals and karate schools would gladly give for free, the program could help build a warrior ethos. Again it's essential to emphasize this wouldn't be some random non-planned program, and the actual implementation would need individual state and district champions working in tandem.

Due to the nature of gym classes already existing, the time we currently have teaching kids kickball and badminton could be converted to a more efficient activity like physical defense training. While karate and martial arts will likely be what most districts call this program, it's important not to lose the end goal. American society needs to accept, train, and expect a certain level of physical violence from its warriors. Saying karate and specific boxing styles for example are nice technicalities. Still, the end state is to create more capable citizens who can prove themselves responsible for using their bodies for their own and collective defense and offense. That requires violence. Upon graduation from the program over the k-12 years, a rite of passage will be a new warrior-capable generation. In turn, this will encourage more military traits like physical ability and discipline, critical skills that will better enable Z to consider service in the armed forces.

Perhaps the scariest form of violence in society today isn't physical, cyber, or even massacres. Instead it's the calls for political violence that have permeated various ideologies. Next we will touch the crucial, controversial, and critical topic of how politics impacts Gen Z military recruiting.

CHAPTER 14:

Protecting The Military From Politics

If there is one thing that Gen Z has grown up with today that wasn't the norm even a decade ago, it's the hyperpolarization of American politics. The fights between the right and left have been intensifying year after year, and the partisanship makes politics a more lurid spectator sport than most N.C.A.A. tournaments. From what books to read in elementary school to what bathrooms to use in adulthood, Z has become accustomed to everyone having an opinion on every political issue. Unique to this generation is that those political thoughts are being discussed online and on television in a more systematic and hostile way than ever before. What used to be reserved for candidate debates or structured discussions has now spilled over into everyday discourse at the dinner table, the Twitter feed, and even the grocery store. Overall, politics does matter to our generation, and we've been so used to hearing about it that it matters more to us than most past generations. However, the military is the last haven of an apolitical workplace and, presented correctly, will be able to attract future employees seeking refuge from the insane state of political discourse.

The first commander-in-chief of the military, George Washington, warned significantly against the power that political parties would come to exert. In his Farewell Address of 1796, he proclaimed, "However [political parties] may now and then answer popular ends, they are likely, in the course of time and things, to become potent engines, by which cunning, ambitious, and unprincipled men will be enabled to subvert the power of the people.[100]" America has a tremendous tradition of civilian control over the military. The armed forces answer to civilian leaders, as all military commanders are ultimately subordinate to a civilian. While this tradition helps keep military power in check, it has unfortunately developed a new and increasingly dangerous tradition of party control of the military. The specific distinction here is that the military answers and should answer to the populace. Still, it should not conduct internal change to satisfy the ruling political parties' immediate whims and wishes. The most powerful military ever assembled is being thrown around like a paper football by the two political parties who are using it to score points in D.C.

If we begin the thought experiment of viewing the military as a business, it's quickly apparent that the current governance structure is unsustainable. The American people are the shareholders in this business. They have ultimate equity and ownership over everything the military does or fails to do in their name. The top Generals and Admirals, along with the executive branch civilians who lead the DoD, are the managers of this business. Above them reside the elected representatives overseeing the military, akin to a board of directors. With a typical board, companies are given strategic guidance with a long-term focus. While managers may come and go, the board's strategic vision helps keep the organization on course despite fads and economic cycles. In our current system, the structure is flipped. The "board" is a body that changes its members and positions every two years in an electoral cycle. Imagine if every time Apple C.E.O.s wanted to extend a vacation plan or create a new promotion title or even put a book on a suggested reading list, they had to convene a heated board meeting open to the public to get approval. The strategic vision on day-to-day management issues is so myopic that it's painfully difficult for our leaders to plan ahead.

While the military is tasked with making plans and projecting future adversary actions on decades-long timeframes, the two political parties are instead acting month-by-month to score political hits. In an ironic twist, this is also the oldest Congress ever, with 23% of its members over 70. It's no wonder there is a disconnect when these discussions about an organization that is skewed to have mostly younger employees, are being held by a body that has only 5% of its members below the age of 35.[101] This domestic conflict between the extreme rhetoric of the Democratic and Republican parties is hurting the military's ability to recruit to fight foreign wars. Imagine a Fortune 500 company manager having to reverse internal policies reflecting people management every other year. The lack of consistency would send the S&P 500 tumbling. This case of parties playing politics is blinding America's most powerful corporation.

Congress should debate the use of our military externally, reacting to world events to determine where we operate and what missions we should undertake. However, the constant back-and-forth micromanagement of policies impacting servicemembers is detrimental to everyone. For many Americans watching on the sidelines, the country may feel more polarized than ever before about what to do with the military. However, that is not the case. "It is a mistake to assume that what is true of Americans who are politically active, also holds true for the greater preponderance of us."[102] The reality is that the polarized political elites on these issues are unrepresentative of the general American public. This is important because the general public is where recruits are drawn from. While there may still be divide and polarization among voters, it is essential to distinguish that it may not be as severe of a divide as the parties will have people believe. Morris Fiorina[103] writes about how the media's selective reporting and overrepresentation of political activists create an atmosphere where the public feels extremely polarized.

As the Republican party fringe pushes the narrative that the military is engaging in "woke" political programs and the Democratic party fringe accuses the military of rampant white supremacy and racism, the average generation-Z voter is confused. Why would they want to join an organization where so many people have such opposing views about what is going on inside it? To further the business analogy presented earlier, the "stock price" and, therefore, the shareholders' valuation should be reflected in the military's actions in defense of the nation. Instead, the two warring political parties are attempting to measure the effectiveness and success of the armed forces by how much their daily H.R. activities align with their professed platforms. When they look at the military through this lens, they neglect to see it as an organization that needs to convince young Gen Zers to serve in it, and instead view it as a way to advance their appeal to voters. In behavioral economics, there's a grand theory known as loss aversion. Loss aversion helps us understand that, psychologically, losses hurt humans more than gains make humans feel good.[104]

Instead of focusing on the tremendous gains the military makes every day to keep America in one of the most peaceful periods in history, the political parties savagely bastardize daily military policies to try and show how this or that action is playing into the other party's hands. Ultimately, the military is accountable to the public and shouldn't be held hostage to the parties' extremes. Generation Z is acutely aware that the average American has more centrist views, and the continued discussion of internal military policy in political debates is turning off would-be recruits.

Generation Z has been calling for this pivot away from the parties in their voting patterns. Harvard Kennedy School's Institute of Politics polls show that Generation Z is one of, if not the, most active youth voting generations in modern history[105]. The polling director of the institute, John Della Volpe, believes that Z represents a fundamental shift in younger-aged involvement in politics. This is a shift much different than what millennials and Gen X'ers brought. Additionally, Zoomers are also less affiliated with political parties than other generations, with "48% calling themselves moderates."[106] Z is instead focused on critical issues that matter to them, and they aren't loyal to a particular party. The mix-and-match culture of the online world doesn't lend itself well to forcing choices into a dipole. Since Zoomers are used to customizing everything from an Amazon t-shirt to an Apple iPhone case, they are heavily confused when they are forced to vote between only two candidates.

Z wants to benefit from mixed thinking. Instead of labeling and then identifying as liberal or conservative, they'd rather discuss ideas on an issue-by-issue basis. The military will never be free from social policy, but these discussions don't have to have party tints. Instead of making short-sighted political changes to the military, a better solution to please Z would be to elongate decision cycles regarding social military policies. This would better match the Overton window and help the military remain the long-term institutional bastion against a tide of quick seasonal change in Washington. Z wants policy but is sick of politics. What this means, in reality, is that the military can and should be presented as the best of both worlds to Zoomers.

It is an organization that views itself as above politics but cares deeply about policy. It's a place where you can't wear your annoying candidate shirts to work or have divisive campaign slogans on your desk. The military grants refuge from the hyper-politicization that the parties are causing in nearly every other workplace in society. Brian Armstrong is the C.E.O. of Coinbase, one of the largest cryptocurrency exchanges. Right before the 2020 election, he published a great no-politics-at-work message to his employees. He remarks that political campaigns within companies hurt them "both by being a distraction, and by creating internal division."[107] The military "C.E.O.s" don't even have to send a speech like this because it is already part of military culture. At the same time, the military touches so many Americans and is an all-encompassing job that policy debates can and should still occur.

From housing to healthcare, the military handles all societal issues. It is a way of life that will inevitably give rise to its members having opinions on which policies are good for them and the country. For too long, we've shied away from open discourse about issues. The culture has promoted silence from its rank and file, but Zoomers see themselves as policy activists. While they might not care about which political hack is championing their causes as much, they want to be heard and feel like they have a say regarding policy. Demanding that no policy be discussed on social media or at work clashes against Gen Zs desire to analyze and then post about their ideas.

A better approach would be allowing Gen Z servicemembers and would-be recruits the transparency and ability to debate political decisions. Take the recent University of Pittsburgh[108] report about the Marine Corps getting rid of the usage of Sir or Ma'am in recruit training. This has caused mass uproar online, and nearly every news agency on the right and left has pounced on this opportunity to offer their opinion.

However, notably absent from these discussions are the current Gen Z service members who have arguably the most stake in its outcome. The military should promote open discussion about policy like this within its ranks of Zoomers. They should be encouraged to post their ideas and thoughts online. This differs from telling or allowing them to support a particular political candidate or party. It also differs from encouraging them to usurp a command decision. You can be a vocal and critical thinker who expresses your beliefs while also falling in line and accepting that you will still obey those in command. Service members should never be in uniform with politicians nor should they deliberately and insubordinately attack senior commanders. Both of these actions undermine the institution and give the perception that our forces are supportive of select ideologies. Still, troops should be included when discussing policy issues that will impact them. The whole country is allowed to rant and rave about policy changes like this, but the current norm of a Marine posting a detailed thought online would get them in serious trouble.

The DoD should do more to give Zers an open voice and a forum to participate in policy debates. Future Zoomers interested in joining the military would look at that favorably. An organization that would allow their voices to be heard and openly accept their policy activism without allowing political party support would be a unique place to work. It would be something filling the void that Z is missing now where workplaces either have an extreme zero politics rule or a hyperpolarized tilt, like many Silicon Valley companies[109].

The approach that should be advocated is a better distinction by the military of what is damaging politics and what is positive policy debate. It may appear as a thin line, but it needs to be delineated. An excellent research paper by Heidi Urben for the National Defense University detailed the armed forces' nonpartisan attempts on social media.[110] One of her findings is that younger military members will use social media for politics more than older members, and that the usage of these online platforms for politics occurs and is not going away anytime soon. So if Gen Z is going to use social media and wants to be political, the military should appeal to them by steering the discussion toward policy and away from partisan parties. This tough balancing act is going to be crucial to appeal to Z.

From an actual implementation standpoint, turning the military into a forum for policy discussion and active thought is going to take push and pull. It will need the "pull" from higher-ups, brave senior leaders (DoD civilians and generals/admirals) to write policy that encourages these discussions. It will take even braver leaders to actually present them to Congress and explain them on T.V. while being grilled. On the "push" side, it will require the next crop of Z military leaders to promote these discussions. In the chow halls, barracks, squad/section rooms, there should be structured time to talk about current events and political ideas that are affecting American military life.

The profound insight here is that the military has the opportunity to emerge as the model for what the rest of society can become. Our organization exists for a clear purpose. It is not a social experiment and it is not a group of like-minded people doing a job. It is both a micro-cosm of larger society and a departure from the normalcy of everyday America. The military sometimes resists certain influences better than other organizations and falls victim to other ones in worse ways. In an

ironic structural twist the military is in some ways a communist organization, run by authoritarians, with the goal of protecting democracy.
We're individuals who work in the same outfit with nearly equal reward
for the betterment of the group, with full command given to one higher
leader, and we fight enemies who threaten the freedom of representative
governments.

What ultimately makes our country's military more powerful than
anything ever seen and different from others in the world is that we
swear an oath to an idea, the Constitution, and not a person. It's often
remarked that adversary leaders fear this very concept, and for that we
must perpetuate the ability to question, debate, and then ultimately
come together on what that idea means in modern day life. Unlike the
trends today of cheering for political figureheads like they're sports stars,
the military can show the way to apolitically analyzing policy ideas that
will steer our country in a better direction. With our unique set of rules,
our people, and our daily work, we can show America what it means to
successfully come together to actually discuss complicated ideas. Yes, it's
natural even for military members to want to identify with one party or
one candidate, but, by putting the oath and the idea above that, we show
a blueprint for how the rest of the country can one day act.

Regarding actual ideological schools of thought, the recruiting
establishment will have to create a careful balancing act. Although the
military at large has a historically slightly conservative tilt (in thought
and voting patterns) and Gen Z at large has a historically slightly progressive tilt (in thought and voting patterns), the DoD is going to have to
figure out how to appeal to Zoomers with more progressive leanings
without alienating the conservative groups that have historically been
overrepresented in the forces. This is no easy task, but the messaging
and policy recommendations can help by being clear-cut. The DoD

should work to keep politics out of the military by weakening the political party's control over the military, and instead encouraging Gen Z to discuss policy issues.

Doing this will increase the bonds formed by those on opposite sides of the political aisle. In society at large, Z's bonds with certain policies are different than those of older generations. Particularly with regard to drugs, Z is taking a new approach. Chapter 15 explains how the military must reanalyze the way it views its relationship with marijuana and alcohol.

CHAPTER 15:
Rethinking Views On Substances

Z oomers spend more time indoors in their places of living than prior
generations. Images of young Americans with eyes glued to video
game consoles and computers come to mind. The entire world took
shelter inside during the pandemic, and social events dropped to nearly
zero. Along with this comes a new view on what recreational activities
are acceptable. Alcohol, the primary social lubricant of the 20th century,
is primarily viewed as declining in popularity compared to its past peaks.
Alcohol is generally consumed in social settings at bars and gatherings,
which decreased due to the lockdown. It also leaves an intense hang-
over that many medical studies are beginning to prove have increasingly

adverse long-term effects. On the other hand, marijuana usage among Z has skyrocketed.

Next to only caffeine, it will likely become this generation's substance of choice. When Elon Musk, the hero to Z who launches rockets and creates electric cars, is seen as cool for smoking weed in a Joe Rogan interview, it's safe to say that this "drug" has become mainstream. Drug usage is one of the big four reasons people are disqualified from joining the military, and weed is the primary driver of that. Although still illegal federally, 21 states now legalized recreational use and 37 have approved medical use. The military should lean into this inevitable trend and not be a laggard on this social issue. The two substances should be treated the same, so fewer people are disqualified or discouraged from joining due to past "drug" use.

Generation Z views alcohol, weed, and drugs as separate categories. Many Zers grew up as the DARE (drug abuse resistance education) program was in effect. DARE and other variants of it were local police-department attempts to educate youth on the dangers of drugs and alcohol. Whether these programs were successes or failures is a big topic of debate, but the language used in them is actually more interesting. Alcohol and drugs. Since Zers watch their parents openly consume alcohol, it was placed in a separate category, while drugs remain this untouchable boogeyman that comprises all other substances. With the legalization laws coming into effect while Z was maturing, things began to shift. More Z parents were openly smoking weed, and the massive rise in cannabis oils, foods, and pens became popular. Z began to mentally separate weed from other, more dangerous drugs.

For the military, however, the devil's lettuce is absolutely forbidden to the point that even talking about it could get you randomly selected for a urinalysis test. The opposite is true of drinking, which is often a primary way of military bonding. Interestingly, younger military members are even more likely to engage in heavy drinking than similar-aged civilians[111]. While not condoned by the military, this heavy drinking is seen as better than one inhalation puff of cannabis. The definition of drugs is a fluid and changing term to Z. In the older half of society that grew up with the cultural revolution of the hippies, drugs inspire fear and banishment. In comparison, the younger half looks at it from a more experimental and nuanced point of view. Not all drugs are the same, nor do they have the same effect. The past generation's battle with nicotine and smoking is a corollary to this.

While cigarettes are also a drug (like weed, they're predominantly smoked), the military used to go so far as to promote smoking breaks on the job. They were part of society, so the military accepted them, arguably even encouraged them. Then, when lots of research came out about their cancerous effects, the military pulled back from them and currently promotes various tobacco cessation programs. However, nearly nobody was disqualified or discouraged from joining the military if they smoked cigarettes. Today the paradigm is flipped. Z is turning to weed as their version of cigarettes. One study even has Cannabis preference as high as 65% compared to alcohol among Zers.[112]

Currently, many mainstream medical circles view it as a curative medicine and stress reliever. Chemicals found in marijuana are now being infused into drinks and food as an entire cannabis industry begins competing for dining dollars.[113] There is a strong chance that as more corporations see a path to make money in the space, increased regulation will push out the more dangerous actors and drug dealers of the past. The cannabis industry will likely become self-regulating like the current alcohol industry. A substance that is almost becoming as commonplace as alcohol and is literally being infused into parts of Zoomer's diets shouldn't be looked at as being in the same group of deadly addictive drugs like opioids such as heroin and cocaine.

Another angle to examine regarding this debate is whether Z's weed usage lowers the pristine standard the military services hold themselves to. We absolutely shouldn't just relax all standards, so our military is filled with less capable warfighters. However, when considering something like weed, the DoD should deeply analyze the results it has on performance. Whereas alcohol has been implicated as a leading culprit in many horrible domestic violence and sexual assault cases, weed is almost rarely seen as a contributor to that. Whereas alcohol significantly impairs decision-making and too many people die each year because of drunkenness, weed's impairment is significantly less fatal, with low overdose rates. In another RAND study, recruits who managed to get a waiver for past marijuana usage didn't perform statistically any worse than non-waivered recruits. Some data even shows they performed better in specific categories.[114] Weed isn't necessarily a superior alternative to alcohol or one that the military should support, but its villainization drives a wedge between the services and the generation.

The all-volunteer force has completely remade itself since Vietnam, and it has fought three major conflicts in the Middle East since. However, many traditions and lessons, good and bad, still linger from that war more than 50 years ago. One of the key issues then was drug abuse among the troops, and Heroin addiction was particularly bad. In a perception-shattering study, Lee Robins documented Heroin use among draftees serving in Vietnam to be as high as 30%. Remarkably it was noted that upon return to a totally different environment in the United States, relapsing dropped to less than a third of that. The finding baffled psychologists questioning how such a powerful trend like this occurred for a drug much more addictive than alcohol or weed.[115] With this, there is the reality that once users were brought to a completely new environment, their addiction rates severely decreased. This is pertinent when analyzing what past marijuana users might do when entering the military. While nobody can make any real argument that modern American life is as stressful or brutal as the jungles of Vietnam during wartime, the point to be noted is that a change in scenery can severely help with substance control.

The same argument can be made that taking a Zoomer who smokes weed either frequently to the point of detriment or simply recreationally will have a fighting chance of giving up that addiction/usage when joining the military. Entry-level boot camp and military training are such a departure from everyday civilian life, that changing the environment hugely benefits breaking bad old habits. The second thing to note from the Heroin findings is how the defense establishment still views drugs through that destructive lens. Heroin is so much more potent, deadly, and addictive that it is safe to say that its use severely hurts troop readiness. A healthy 18-year-old who smokes weed occasionally isn't any less ready or able to fight than one who drinks a few beers weekly. Changing the mindset of being more accepting of past and even some current weed usage isn't an actual compromise of standards.

There are a few fundamental recommendations that the military can implement to improve its overall view on marijuana usage. Firstly, all recruiter questions about past usage should cease. While other drug and drug offenses should still require waivers and deeper investigation, no weed questions should continue. This would remove the need for waivers for those who have self-disclosed weed usage. The stigma associated with the DoD's views on drugs makes many believe they are already disqualified due to their past actions. There's also the severity question. Due to the binary way the military views weed, *any* weed usage technically has to be reported, even just a few experimental times. Lumping heavy addicts with recreational smokers is, again, too broad of an approach that doesn't correctly solve the issue. If the military doesn't move to full acceptance, then at least a partial gradient distinguishing intensity of use should be employed. From an internal policy standpoint post-joining, weed should be treated with the same level of severity as alcohol.

To actually implement this, there are a few paths to take. The quickest and most public way would be for Congress to pass regulating legislation in the National Defense Authorization Act. Short of that, each service branches' individual recruiting commands could write policy to change recruiters' screening of this issue. Since this is also technically a medical issue, MEPS (the military entrancing processing stations) would also have to be looped in and supportive of the idea. Finally, individual front-line recruiters (some of whom may possibly do this already) could make the painfully difficult ethical decision of ignoring past usage or simply not inquiring about it. Changes in a bureaucracy are never easy, but at some point in the chain it has to come, or else we will continue to miss out on thousands of otherwise qualified candidates.

To further this new thinking, barracks inspections would remove weed-linked contraband items, but they would no longer be grounds for dismissal or imprisonment. Alcohol reduction programs would likewise have supporting marijuana portions and would be able to actively counsel and discuss cannabis instead of pretending like nobody uses it. The intrusive and inefficient amount of urinalysis tests that occur in schoolhouses and randomly during training should only be testing for hard drugs and more addictive substances. They should not screen for weed at all. With all that change, which may seem radical to some seasoned servicemembers, lines will still have to be drawn in the sand. Any suspected weed usage at work or being high during working hours cannot be met without some punishment. Similar to how alcohol use at work is a current no-go, the strong cultures of peer accountability will be able to detect and prevent this from occurring.

Lastly, the drinking age for alcohol itself should be relaxed for service members. A current public restriction that makes the drinking age in the U.S. three years later than most other countries can present the opportunity for a recruiting perk. As an added benefit of joining the military, local, state, and federal governments should allow bar entry and alcohol consumption to all active duty service personnel with valid government I.D.s. While underage drinking is already a phenomenon that occurs anyway, society plays this silly game pretending like you have to wait until you reach twenty-one. This legal drinking restriction puts America far behind Europe on binge drinking issues. It creates all sorts of dangerous practices like heavy consumption in private barracks rooms before heading for a night out.

As an officer, you're often tasked with sitting duty. Many wild things happen on duty, most of which involve some sort of alcohol influence. Once, I witnessed a barracks party with copious amounts of drinking and alcohol. I also felt empathy for these young service members who had no unsupervised place to themselves to have an enjoyable time. In the past, the military worried about drunk driving off base and therefore had a stronger desire to keep troops from driving out into town. With the abundance of Uber and ride-sharing services, that risk is safely mitigated. The situation is exactly flipped where it is probably safer drinking together in a public and open bar rather than sneaking from the duty officer in government quarters.

If young recruits can't have the same experience many of their similar-aged peers are having in college, the least we can do is allow them to enjoy some of the freedoms of adulthood. In short, relaxing the drinking policy and promoting a potential perk that if you join the military, you can go to a bar, would be a step in the right direction.

To be clear, nobody is arguing that the military should champion the use of alcohol or marijuana. There is no question that these substances have adverse health, psychological, and some performance effects. There will hopefully remain a solid social stigma around using and abusing these substances in the military culture. With that noted, the DoD needs to heavily reexamine how it treats the recruiting pool regarding marijuana. It should stop frequent random testing for usage, and in recruiting it should treat weed in a similar manner that it treats alcohol. It's important to draw the distinction that there will never be open talk of weed smoking like there is of alcohol drinking. Marijuana will likely remain federally illegal for a long time. Still, the consumption and experimentation with the substance can no longer be used as this massive knife that severely cuts in the eligible recruiting pool.

Furthermore, the drinking age should be lowered to 18 for those in uniform as a perk of serving the country. It should be a just vote of confidence that those responsible for defense have earned the right to drink alcohol. Allowing for a loosening of restrictions always strikes fear in an orderly, discipline-based organization. Choosing what to loosen and to what effect remains the struggle of every military leader. However updating the marijuana and alcohol policy is an easy recruiting win that brings much more reward than risk.

Along the lines of supporting the changing habits of Generation Z, there is one category that has become more detrimental to our growth than anything else. The mental health epidemic that has swept our generation is a continuing problem that the military must get out in front of.

CHAPTER 16:
Coping With Issues Of the Mind

While the physical health of Gen Z tracks with previous age-groups, their overall mental health is suffering immensely. Gen Z is likely the most anxious and depressed American generation, as the constant influx of a digital life takes its toll. In past human history, we've suffered from issues of scarcity, like not having enough food and being bored. Now we suffer from issues of abundance like having too many high-fructose foods and stimulation overloads. We've been given everything, so our lack of wanting inevitably leads to a lack of meaning. Viktor Frankl, a concentration camp survivor wrote the most remarkable book on this topic titled *Man's Search for Meaning.* He says, "What man actually needs is not a tensionless state but rather the striving and struggling for a worthwhile goal, a freely chosen task."[116] As Z searches for meaning in an overindulged society, their mental health is deteriorating at an increasingly alarming rate. The military must recognize that the younger population needs more mental rather than physical health support.

The current Z mental state is not good. Compared to Boomers, Gen Z had 19% more reported loneliness.[117] Suicide is the second-highest cause of death for Z, as the CDC reported a tragic 56% increase in the act from 2007 to 2017[118] among young Americans. Rates of body dysmorphia that lead to general eating disorders such as anorexia and bulimia have skyrocketed to staggering numbers. With everyone able to portray a picture-perfect life online, seeing past the masks of filters usually reveals struggle and sadness. Even the entertainment we watch, like *The Boys, Black Mirror,* and *Everything Everywhere All at Once,* has an alarmingly high rate of nihilism.

Coupled with this extreme rise in mental illness has been an increased search for solutions. Some creative Zers are actually "going retro" to connect with the simpler past. One trend has seen Zers buy vintage flip phones without all the constant connectivity a standard iPhone brings. This behavior shows some desire to turn back the clock and have easier times and calmer mental states. The popular app BeReal demands an untouched photo of people that is posted quickly, so they don't continuously obsess over appearance editing. A third phenomenon has been the growth of guided meditation apps, as the practice has a growing following among Zoomers.

While these are positive and creative ways to deal with the issue, a far more sinister medically administered solution is usually the go-to treatment: overmedication. With potentially 42% of Zers having some mental health condition, upwards of 57% of those diagnosed are taking some form of medication for it.[119] Here the statistical numbers paint an increasingly bleak story. While mental health is indeed talked about more and perhaps diagnosed more, the drug treatment explosion is legitimately altering Z's minds. The opioid epidemic that has plagued various regions of the country is an extension of this issue, not to mention the cocktail of uppers used to aid a generation that has some of its members stuck in perpetual gloom.

In Z's eyes, the military, which formerly was a breeding ground for strong self-confidence and willpower, has become a place where mental health is even worse than in civilian society. While the military has always faced its own challenges due to the nature of the dangerous work it performs, troops are even more at risk based on recent data. In 2022, four Navy sailors at one facility died by suicide within just a few short weeks.[120] For the first time in combat history, 21st-century servicemembers are more likely to die by self-inflicted suicide than battle wounds. The current mind struggles faced by service members who fought in Iraq and Afghanistan have been well documented. Z has grown up watching the PTSD scars from deployments. For a generation already grappling with depression, joining an organization whose work seemingly exacerbates that becomes a major turn-off.

The PTSD crisis that Z watched afflict millennial veterans is often viewed as the result of combat trauma and the horrors of being so close to killing. Eliott Ackerman, former Marine and author of *Green on Blue* and *2034*, explains, "there is this other type of PTSD that I would kind of correlate with just this, this purposelessness, this inability to find meaning outside of the war".[121] Many returning Veterans struggled with adapting to mundanity and the lack of purpose in civilian life that so many Zers also feel. This is one of the key issues in a tech-abundant world and one that close military connections to listening and caring peers can help alleviate.

To begin to wrap solutions around such a massive and society-wide problem is not easy, but the military has an excellent place to start. Through Tricare, the servicemembers' healthcare system, all troops are given free medical care. The dual mission of Tricare involves supporting deployed troops overseas while keeping them combat-ready and healthy when back home. Tricare is a great benefit, and VA health supports older veterans. But younger Z military members need more mental rather than physical healthcare. Currently, the system is set up like a typical medical provider focusing primarily on bodily issues. As humans age, they naturally have more of these and go to the doctor more. However, healthy young Zers aren't rushing to clinics for knee, back, or heart pain quite as frequently. Sure, they still get physical injuries and have medical emergencies, but not nearly at the same rate as older Americans. So, the system must change to start with a mental focus first upon the initial joining of the force.

The budget is strained, and allocations need to be made somewhere, but prioritizing the mind in the beginning and the body as the life cycle progresses optimizes impact from a utilitarian perspective. A lot more Zers who are under 25 and struggling with their first experiences away from home need mental support before they deal with the common physical ailments that come with older age. Suppose we can shift the overall mindset of military health, to begin with the mental before the bodily. In that case, we can start to get tactical in solving Z's problems with anxiety and depression.

Paradoxically, with more "friends" than ever, we feel more alone. Not everyone has that person to help them through the most challenging times. The DoD has recognized this issue and started some initiatives toward making the force a more mentally hospitable workplace. That said, our work will always be challenging, and a lot of change is yet to be implemented to improve the military's mental health image. The newly passed Brandon Act now allows for confidential mental health reporting. This is a good start, but still more drastic investment is needed to fundamentally change the issue that is seemingly gripping the entire generation. I look back on college when we had a slew of suicides on campus. There was a horrible irony that this could happen even at one of the best funded Ivy League schools in the country. We were complete with tremendous resources, and one of the largest hospitals in the U.S. was actually part of our campus. Indeed, the director of our university's mental health counseling department himself committed suicide, proving literally anyone can be at risk. There's no perfect solution to solving this multifaceted problem, but within the military training as many Gen Z peers as possible to be mental health advocates is a better way that we can effectively cover our mental "six."

In addition, there exists a critical untapped asset to help combat this crisis: combat medics. The concept of sending Army medics and Navy corpsmen with frontline troops arose in WWII. The Imperial Japanese even mocked the idea, calling the care with which we go to preserve life a sign of weakness. From Hacksaw Ridge to Hamburger Hill, brave Americans who have administered care on the battlefield have been immortalized in popular films. These professionals are not licensed nurses but instead complete basic medical training and operate more like medical technicians. The safety they provide and the skills they acquire through experience make them extremely valuable in hostile environments.

The way to truly get the most out of them would be to similarly employ them in domestic environments, too. Hiring more nurses or doctors may not be feasible, but these primary care providers can fill the gap if empowered to do so.[122] By encouraging the addition of a training pipeline in mental health, these medics/corpsmen can begin to be the first line of support against suicidal tendencies and mental illness. While perhaps everyone should be given more robust training to assist military brothers and sisters who are struggling, those who have already chosen the medical field will naturally be more inclined to offer aid. Assigning specific technicians with specific units and keeping them engaged to the point that they know their people are essential. It will facilitate trust and their ability to act as quasi-counselors/therapists in the mental health war.

Lastly, the solution to tech-induced mental health may ironically come from tech itself. Since COVID prevented many in-person doctor visits, telehealth and telemedicine rapidly filled the gap. The ability to provide care virtually is a great force multiplier for an already overworked Tricare staff. Mental health is the perfect candidate to tackle with this because diagnoses and verbal treatment therapies often happen via words. While some of this already exists, it does not trickle down effectively to the junior level. There is no easy pipeline for junior enlisted troops to talk to therapists online. Above that, whatever exists is hardly discussed and is not yet part of the military culture. Z itself has to be the difference maker. Continued discussion and awareness of these issues among the current Z service community are crucial to reverse this catastrophe. Only then will future joiners see the military as a place that prioritizes mental health. Suppose the mindset shifts to where we can accept that emotional distress can make people just as combat ineffective as physical injury. In that case, there will be a proper reallocation of medical resources. By emphasizing mental first as new Zers enter the force, future service-members will begin to understand that the military is back on track to providing a great place to work.

We now conclude part three's discussion about how social and cultural issues impact Gen Z and military recruitment. In part four, I will take a zoomed out macro view to discuss how the military as an organization can better give back to society at large.

Promoting Ways In Which the Military Can Give Back to Society

My Marine Corps training began during a strange time period. While thousands of Marine Officers have been tested over the years, the new crop of Zers were the first to do so with masks on. Even our isolated base environment wasn't spared as the COVID-19 pandemic altered nearly all aspects of the outside world. With my face covered with an N95, it dawned on me then just how powerful collective human behavior can be. Large and well organized groups of people have and will continue to change the world for the better or worse depending on their leadership and guidance.

Towards the very end of our training, as masks were lifted, we participated in a week-long field exercise called WarFex. Many stressful decisions and learning lessons occurred that could fill an entire book, but one moment stands out. It was boiling hot in the Quantico swamp, and we were given the order to seize a fortified city at 10:00 AM. We had strong intel that another platoon would also be attacking the city at the same time, so it was a race between the two of us to get the positional advantage. However, it was day three, and we had not yet had any water resupply, so many Marines were "in the black on water." This means they were cramping and beginning to near dehydration. We had two water filtration bladders and were instructed to find and filter our water from one of the few running streams in the terrain. Upon reaching our first identified stream, our morale sank as we saw that it was completely dry. The commanding officer of the Basic School had given us an inspiring speech saying, "people have found a way to take the situation you're complaining about and win," so I decided to have us continue our hike until we found another stream. This one was supposed to be the most flowing stream on the map, but it was a stagnant trickle of muddy water when we arrived. "What now, Lieutenant?" one of my peers asked me, as the environmental situation directly harmed our survivability.

Part four concludes the work by looking at ways that the powerful force of the military can be used for the good of society. It touches on issues such as workplace representation, community involvement, and the environment. I argue that some of our societal ills that are so talked about today may need to be solved from the largest organization we have at our disposal. It concludes with a call for action as we gear up for what may be a very conflict-intensive decade with near-peer competitors.

CHAPTER 17:

Becoming Bigger Parts in Local Communities

An area of the economy that has grown exponentially during Gen Z's rise has been the sharing economy. Also described as "gig-work" such as ride services like Uber and apartment rentals like Airbnb, Zoomers are accustomed to interacting freely with strangers. Over 30% of U.S. adults aged 18-29 report having done some gig work.[123] Furthermore, a majority report spending less than 10 hours in a typical week performing these tasks. This increase in fluid interactions has promoted a much more inter-connected community. While the tenet that "every person's home is their castle" still rings true in the American psyche, a more modern, Z-adapted view of communal life would be that "a castle can't exist without a group."

Z is the first actual "co" generation where popular trends like coworking and co-living are becoming the norm. The local communities where they're from, where they choose to live, and where they work are meaningful to them because, now more than ever, young people rely on the larger community to achieve their daily goals and tasks. It follows that serving these communities is something that Z values intensely, and many Zers expect their jobs to have some level of community service. It has become a social mark of approval to be a Zer who "gives a s###" and does community service. Gen-Z wants to feel good by being seen as virtuous and serving others. First by increasing contact between the military and civilian sectors, and then by having the military serve the civilian communities that they interact with; the military can show how they give back to their local communities to attract more recruits.

Local coworking spaces should be taken advantage of to increase military-civilian interaction. One particularly unique aspect of the American military is that it takes citizens from all parts of our vast nation and concentrates them in specific pockets of domestic garrison bases. While different-sized bases exist throughout the country, the towns they exist in often bifurcate into two camps. Part of the local towns surrounding the base become complete extensions of the military. They usually comprise military families living closely off base and often are worked in by the non-uniformed spouse. These subcommunities have barbers, supply shops, and gyms that create a micro-economy catering specifically to the armed services. Fort Hood in Texas and the surrounding town of Killeen are perfect examples of this. Then there exists the other camp. The farther parts of town have absolutely no connection to the military base that exists in or near it. Perhaps the base is too small or too far away, but besides faint reminders that the military shares a home here, there is almost no impact on the local community. Most New Yorkers would be hard-pressed to recall that there exists an active Fort Hamilton in Brooklyn.

Young, unmarried service members are mandated to live on base in barracks, and they don't get the same community immersion as older, married service members. However, in many of these same base-agnostic American communities, ample physical space exists to encourage the interchange of ideas between the military and the local populace. Coworking has exploded in the United States, with the nation leading the world in the number of built spaces. Initially designed for entrepreneurs to cheaply rent temporary offices on short timelines, the model of sharing desks and communal areas has created positive network effects for all sizes of companies. From two Zoomers working on a startup in college to a marketing firm with 100 employees, having different companies on the same office floor has yielded great emotional and economic benefits. People who belong to coworking spaces often report levels of thriving higher than people who don't[124].

While field training and particular military work won't be able to take place anywhere but on base, other administrative jobs can "hot desk" in local community coworking centers. Having rented space for troops to get off base and do studies or extra work on Fridays, would be a step in the right direction toward integrating more fully with local communities. This would increase interaction that could then lead to service. Z wants to engage with the communities they're working in. Having speakers at these coworking spaces or doing community service work out of them alongside civilians will increase innovation and connection. Busing a platoon of soldiers to a community service site to take a few feel-good photos is a thing of the past. Instead, working to assist in a local after-school curriculum redesign, alongside civilians of similar ages in a sleek office space, is the community service of the future.

Housing policy in the military should be altered to promote more integration into local communities. The DoD currently owns or leases over 395 million square feet of family housing, making it the largest category of physical property that the DoD controls.[125] In recent years, a slew of reporting has shed light on some of the horrors associated with military housing. With black mold and other structural damages, it has become commonplace to hear of criminal developers and landlords taking advantage of families' living situations. Reuters[126] released a bombshell report showing how one major landlord, Balfour Beatty, had employees systematically fudging maintenance reports and other records to pocket millions in bonuses while lying to the military. Thousands of servicemembers and their children have had permanent health problems due to these abuses of their living spaces. It's important to mention that some excellent landlords and home maintenance companies are dedicated to serving the military community. Often smaller, more niche owners who are Veterans are excellent landlords who provide great care to their properties. These smaller owners are often stewards of one or two properties and use their advantageous VA loans to own real estate and generate side income. They should be rewarded and prized as true friends of active duty troops.

There is currently no "Better Business Bureau" equivalent for active-duty housing, but the local bases should push to produce socially verified lists of which properties/owners can be trusted and which have issues. Still, there has to be a better solution than what exists with the current traditional model. Co-living offers something unique that would allow military members to better integrate into American towns. Co-living models where individual dorm-like rooms share various amenities, like a communal kitchen or study space, are popping up everywhere. The initial impetus for many Zoomers moving to large cities is to save on rent by opting for this cheaper living arrangement. However, the social benefits of living and sharing among similar-aged people are why the Zers stay in these communities. Robert Pinnegar, C.E.O. of the National Apartment Association, writes that for Z, "A walkable community with easy access to entertainment, dining, shopping and a gym is another necessity among this demographic."[127] Co-living is an affordable way for Z to share space and mix with others in the community. Still, there would likely be stiff resistance to an innovative idea like this.

For one, barracks for entry-level recruits are government property and provide the military with increased authority over what goes on in those spaces (e.g., health and welfare inspections). Additionally, the easy access to a chow hall and a centralized location of all troops make daily administrating much easier. As many single service members progress through the ranks, they begin looking off-base for housing. They immediately rush to shared rentals or on-base housing options because they are all that exist. Instead, with the help of the DoD, the co-living concept needs to permeate the areas surrounding the base and select spots on base. If a newly built co-living apartment complex went up on base and were open cheaply to local citizens not affiliated with the military (who'd be given a base-entry pass), there would be community members living in that complex along with servicemembers. Likewise, if a co-living complex were built right near the base and marketed not just to civilians but also military members, the living interactions there would benefit both groups. The Zers would have another touchpoint with the community and would be able to figure out more ways to give back to it.

Having more friends and acquaintances in the local cities would make Zers in uniform more aware of how their work actions directly benefit everyday Americans. It would also help remove the alienation many Zers feel when they move to these new communities. Gone should be the days when bases are these hidden enclaves that are out of sight and out of mind. When we allow junior military members to live in isolation from society in a forced location, it reduces the connection this community-minded generation has to the very types of towns and cities they hailed from. Very few other jobs require forced living with coworkers and only coworkers. Allowing for a more normal living arrangement with civilians would be a great boon for the military and the local community. Housing policy needs to show Z that when you join the military, you can be a good neighbor and have regular civilian neighbors.

I personally benefited from the community aspects of co-living during my time in Washington, D.C. Having moved to the city in the midst of the pandemic, the loneliness and inability to meet people were difficult. Luckily, my building had shared living where I met a new roommate and group of friends. Although we worked in totally separate portions of the economy and would likely have never met otherwise, we became modern versions of neighbors and created a sense of community in a time everyone needed it.

Overall, by harnessing the trends of coworking and co-living, the military can better integrate with the communities it supports. It shouldn't be lost that while the entire country is a shareholder in the corporation known as the DoD, the local communities that bases exist in are also prominent stakeholders. In the report "Commander's Guide to Community Involvement," commanders are encouraged and recommended to get involved in the community via service organizations.[128] The young force of Z volunteers recruited into the armed services every year is eager to donate time and service to causes in the communities they move into. The current disconnect is how to facilitate this urge for community service when young recruits often live and work in places very separate from civilian life. When service members are frequently asked to move from location to location every few years, the switching costs of having to re-acclimate are a challenge. Support groups and base adjustment programs have existed for decades, but the lack of permanency makes it hard to establish roots and form networks with locals. Many services have explored the concept of homesteading, which tries to enable servicemembers to spend longer parts of their careers in one location. Regardless, increased interaction with local citizens would allow cooperative learning exchanges and opportunities to hear about volunteering.

Volunteering happens due to potential volunteers' proximity to current volunteers. In a case study done on "The Impact of A Military Base On Community Volunteering," it was found that "the most significant number of base personnel volunteering (44%) were asked to do so by someone at work and another 20% reported being asked by a friend."[129] Coworking, in reality, is a perfect place for this networking to occur. One peer-reviewed definition of coworking is actually "an organic form of 'connected learning' - a model that regards learning as an *interest-driven* and *socially embedded* experience."[130] Overall, the military can promote service and demonstrate to Zoomers that they can impact their local communities while in uniform, by harnessing the powerful trends of coworking and coliving. Service to these communities while in the armed forces helps create easier pipelines for integrating back into them after troops decide to take the uniform off. There is no reason that, while in the US, military members should be completely ripped out of society when they're expected to reintegrate into it one day. Instead, living, working, and promoting service projects with their civilian peers will help show future Zers how beneficial the military can be.

Regarding civilian peers, one particular group stands out in terms of who the military should be marketed and represented to. Women make up over half of society, yet their military participation rates are dramatically low. The next chapter will explore how women can present a great opportunity and solution to the recruiting crisis.

CHAPTER 18:

Fostering a Better Environment for Females in Uniform

Before I delve into this critical discussion about women in the military, I want to recognize that conversations on identity and beliefs are often sensitive. As a straight white male, I bring my own biases and blind spots to this analysis. However, most of the military consists of straight white males, and we should all be encouraged to share our thoughts and ideas openly and democratically. These thoughts shouldn't be tempered at all for the risk of offending someone or hurting feelings. They should have the utmost respect for fundamental human rights and fellow-human emotions. Still, we shouldn't be so afraid in modern times to have painful, "politically incorrect" discussions, that we fail to reach the best outcomes for all. In order for our society and our institution to function, we must be able to talk about groups that we aren't a part of without being shouted down. Gen Z is much more realistic than the idealistic millennials, and our collective pessimism makes us want to engage in challenging conversations, even if they sting a little.

Another thing to clarify is the difficult job of toeing the line that recruitment organizations will have to do as we push the military forward. Just because, on average, Zoomers lean more in one direction or have newer ideas about societal constructs than older generations, it doesn't mean that the entire Generation Z is a monolith. If too much change is pushed too quickly, there is a risk of alienating many of the groups of thinkers who were past mainstays of the recruiting pool. Striking a balance and doing everything in moderation are the best way. These changes and discussions must happen often, in public, and be positively tempered to reach optimality for total force numbers, abilities, and ultimately lethality.

As the military searches for new ways to connect to the American populace, one group stands far above the others as key to answering this problem. A Council on Foreign Relations report proclaims, "When the draft ended in 1973, women represented just 2 percent of the enlisted forces and 8 percent of the officer corps. Those numbers are 16 percent and 19 percent, respectively, significantly increasing over the past half-century."[131] Our military has become more accepting and open to women over the past years. However, we are nowhere near where we should be. With nearly half of the U.S. workplace, and around two-thirds of college enrollees, being female,[132] the dismal comparative numbers in the armed forces are lackluster. With women breaking glass ceilings in many sectors of society, the military should not be left out of capitalizing on this remarkable surge of talent. That being said, the military is unique to every other industry in society, and its special work poses different challenges toward integration. Women are the largest group of Gen Z that can and should be recruited more into the military. To do that, the military should employ the HER framework: honoring gender differences, eradicating sexual assault, and relaxing female-specific social constraints.

Honoring gender differences is a crucial component to increasing female generation-Z recruitment. Most surveys report that many Zers view gender as a more fluid spectrum rather than a hard-cut binary. So while this doesn't necessarily encompass the majority, there is at least a large enough group with a different relationship with gender than in the past. The DoD must recognize this in how it presents gender to the recruitment pool. However, regardless of opinions or feelings on gender, there exist scientifically documented, unique biological and neurochemical differences between those born with two X chromosomes and those born with an X and a Y chromosome. For the vast majority of human history in the vast majority of civilizations, the act of fighting wars was performed by men. While the contributions of women to various war efforts should not be diminished, when zooming out to take a much longer historical perspective, it has been extremely rare for women to be in military uniform and participate in direct activities closely related to battle.

While modern times have successfully unlocked women's tremendous and often superior power to perform jobs and tasks, we shouldn't be immediately seeking full numerical parity in every role the military has to offer. Many women can and will do certain jobs better than men, but it is important to look at averages when dealing with the macro problem of recruiting. Some job roles consistently show that men are better than women, while other roles like aircraft mechanics, educators, and caregivers show, on average, women far surpassing men. We've become so afraid of offending each other that we're walking on eggshells around these thorny issues instead of diving in to attack them head-on.

Take the analogy of a math major and an English major applying for a job at Facebook. It would seem silly to assume that both of these candidates had the same skill sets and the same desired job roles. People often study what they're good at, so it would be logical to conclude that the English major was, on average, a better writer, while the math major was, on average, better with numbers. Appealing to the English major to apply for an editing role at Facebook while appealing to the math major to apply to a software engineering role would seem logical, acceptable, and fair. In the military, we seemingly can't discuss these things any more or risk being called misogynistic or out-of-touch. We should all be champions of women who break the gender barrier and take on increasingly physically demanding roles like those in the infantry. However, targeting women to join the infantry is a misallocation of scarce resources. The data shows that, on average, they struggle more with training and job performance. This indisputable fact shouldn't trigger anyone or discourage the brave and legendary women who serve in the infantry.

Still, it should be a clear-cut wake-up call that the average woman can make more impact and perform superior to men in other fields. All the time and money spent focusing on the flashy debate surrounding women in combat roles doesn't prioritize getting more women in uniform and benefitting from their unique abilities and talents. Instead, the differences and aptitudes between the sexes should be recognized, celebrated, and put to good use. For example, women were found to be more effective than men in 84% of leadership competencies measured.[133] They are also, on average, better writers and readers.[134] A simple follow-on to this would be that military jobs prioritizing reading/writing should be shown more to women recruit groups.

Recruiting must focus on improving the general outlook of how women are treated as equals in a force that pays and promotes based on merit, not gender. With the rise of Transgenderism, the debate over pronouns and whether drill instructors can be called Sir and Ma'am is also occurring. These are complex societal questions that fire up emotions on both sides and are beyond the scope of this book. I will however delicately argue that this hot-button issue is distracting from the much larger recruiting pool that should be focused on. While working to make a proper role for transgenders in the military should be a noble and deeply researched goal, it garners way too much media attention, political debate, and command decision-making time for what is a relatively small percentage of recruitable Zers. Instead, from a purely military standpoint, more Z women by birth need to be recruited so that the DoD can benefit from their unique thinking and abilities. The way to recruit them is to respect the differences they bring to the table and recognize that they should be given a choice to be exposed to different recruiting strategies and job paths than those traditionally meant for men.

The second part of the HER framework involves eradicating sexual assault. Until the military becomes a safe and accepting place for women, there will be no chance of increasing female recruitment. For a generation who grew up witnessing the #MeToo movement, sexual assault prevention is of key importance to both male and female Zoomers. The Annual Report on Sexual Assault in the Military[135] saw a horrific 13% increase in sexual assault reports this past year. There is a genuine, palpable feeling that women are at higher risk of sex crimes in the armed forces. Until these assaults are stopped, and that perception is ameliorated, a large swath of Gen Z women will not look favorably on military service. After the tragic murder of Vanessa Guillen, her family, along with a brave few in Congress, moved mountains to get her eponymous bill passed. The law moves prosecution jurisdiction outside the victim's chain of command and helps protect sexual abuse reporters from retaliation. While this is a significant step forward, the military still lags behind many private sector firms dealing with this issue, and it's somewhat of a mystery why.

There is some credence to suggest that due to the nature of military activities, troops are more prone to unwanted sexual incidents. The "full lifestyle" of the military, which sees people in very stressful situations in very close proximity, is a much more physical and intimate type of contact than private sector jobs. Although this may appear vulgar to the elder classes of think tanks and bureaucrats, who like conducting sanitized, statistical surveys about the military, the ground truth is much rougher than expected. Recruit and combat training (even basic barracks life) is such a physical, mental, and emotional departure from normal society that those who haven't experienced it will struggle to understand what it is like.

The over-sexualization of Gen-Z music and movies only exacerbates this. Sex is talked about a lot. The isolation from potential partners in society, coupled with a general lack of privacy, causes intense sexual deprivation among many young troops. While this is no excuse for horrific and unacceptable sexual crimes (and those horrible occurrences must be treated with the strongest punishments), there is no clean-cut solution to fix this situation. Silly proposals from ivory towers imploring young men to simply "act better" are useless. Although the answer remains unclear, it should be the top priority of all commands to eradicate sexual assault. Each battalion/squadron-sized organization in the military should have its sexual assault/harassment statistics publicly published on the DoD homepage. This way each year, the public could view each commander's leadership and cast a solid moral shadow over those who've failed to prevent these acts from occurring.

The final leg of the HER framework involves relaxing female-specific social constraints. The military is showing great flexibility in relaxing various grooming and personal appearance standards in the past year. For a fighting force that has traditionally had a hard-cut mandate on appearance, more tattoo waivers and looser hair restrictions are emerging trends leaders are coming around to. For Gen Z, self-expression is essential. Fashion and appearance matter more now than ever as the world exposes us to a wider variety of aesthetic trends. While certain uniformity helps enforce discipline, allowing for piercings while not on duty and continuing to allow for new hairstyles among females will enable the military to compete for talent with other jobs. We may not yet be ready for hair dyed green in a mohawk, but we should allow more males and females who want to express themselves in various appearances.

Another unique social constraint facing military females is the stigma around fraternization and dating. Fraternization currently prohibits certain relationships between officers and enlisted, an outdated rule tied to an old tradition of the 1700s. While any workplace will suffer problems if dating occurs between people who work closely together, fraternization should only apply to those in the same unit or the same direct chain of command. Additionally, dating between service members is often met with stigma and contempt. When finding partners, Zoomers have turned to what they know best—their iPhones. Tinder, Hinge, and Bumble are three of the most popular dating apps used by a generation that prefers flirting with emojis rather than drinks at a bar. These apps work great when there is a high population of similar-aged potential mates nearby. For entry-level military recruits, their strict schedules, isolated locations, and inability to bring strangers home in government-owned barracks break the algorithm's effectiveness.

In fact, due to the increased pay and ability to live off base, many new servicemembers get married exceptionally young. Compared to similar-aged civilians, young service members are more than three times more likely to have spouses[136]. The current way these pay and freedom incentives are set up encourages early marriages to the detriment of more extended dating periods and sometimes more carefully planned decisions. If would-be female warriors, with a quicker biological clock for having children, look at the military and reason they won't be able to have outside romantic relationships, fewer would-be warriors turn into actual warriors. To this end, the military should look at relaxing its internal dating standards and constraints around supporting nonmarital romantic relationships. At a minimum, rebalancing the playing field away from how it currently favors married relationships would be a start. For example, perhaps a young service member begins a romantic relationship with someone in town. If that relationship turned into something more serious, he/she would be allowed to live with their boyfriend/girlfriend off base. This would extend the benefit/option of living on their own without forcing instant marriage, thus allowing those two individuals the opportunity to understand their relationship first.

My younger sister is one of the most impactful people in my life. I often look at her and wonder if I would recommend the military to her. As a smart, athletic, and great leader I know she'd thrive in our force. Yet, due to some of the various cultural issues I just mentioned, I don't yet know if I would fully support her putting on a uniform. As tough and personal as that is to admit, I am optimistic that Zoomers will be the generation where we change that to the point where I'd give a resounding thumbs-up on her taking the oath.

By following the HER framework, the military can begin to bridge the gender divide that is holding it back. By honoring gender differences, eradicating sexual assault, and relaxing female-specific social constraints, the DoD will begin to attract more Gen-Z women into its ranks.

While women represent the single largest group the DoD must focus on regarding recruiting, attracting other Zers in a multitude of groups is also an absolute must. Next we will discuss ways the military can boost its diversity at large.

CHAPTER 19:

Drawing from America's Unique Heterogeneous Tapestry

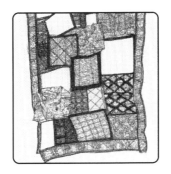

The military is no stranger to acronyms. We likely have more than any other organization in the world. They serve an excellent purpose when used tactically to abbreviate long-worded actions over the radio. Our fellow citizens in the civilian sector understandably aren't as good at making acronyms with actionable meanings. They sometimes clump together drastically different nouns in the hope that they coalesce around one central message, often accidentally obfuscating the individual words. During my summer internship at Goldman Sachs, the senior partners had some of us junior Zers work on defining ESG since it was the raging new topic for Wall Street investing. When putting together our final presentation decks, we discovered that while people do care about environmental, social, and governance issues when they put money into companies, the three words as a whole have very little to do with each other.

More than this, there is a new buzz acronym that is generating controversy and discussion amongst employers: DEI, standing for diversity, equity, and inclusion. While similar and certainly related, it's important to break down what each of these words mean. Especially for organizations and leaders unfamiliar with these concepts, it will be important to understand that each word is a separate Gen Z demand for their workplace and larger society. The concepts are related, and their relationships to each other matter. So I will explore each word in isolation and in connection. Overall, they call for a process of seeing the difference, understanding the difference, and accepting the difference among fellow Americans.

Diversity is about seeing the difference. Diversity debates can cause rage nowadays to the point that even mentioning the word can create anger and confusion. From a first-principles standpoint, America has been and will always be the "melting pot" of the world. We are unique because we're a place where different people have moved to seek freedom. This difference is the polar opposite of China, the nation that today represents the greatest threat to that very same freedom. Where we don't have size-of-population advantages, we do have uniqueness-of-population advantages. That being said, these differences among our population sometimes present unique obstacles in working together. Although one of the most diverse and multicultural nations on earth, America consistently ranks highest in one specific behavioral trait: individualism.

Individualism boosts innovation in good economic times but severely hampers collective action during times of challenge.[137] This individualistic spirit is even further pronounced among Zoomers, who represent the most diverse generation America has ever had. Past chapters have already touched on gender, political, religious, geographic, socioeconomic, and even age diversity. However, the more traditional definition of the word diversity usually revolves around racial, ethnic, sexual identity, and cultural diversity. Regardless, diversity at its core represents variety and, like its root word, difference. The minute three people work together to form a group, there can be countless differences among them to create numerous categories of diversity. It's up to society and the military to successfully determine which diverse categories matter to help channel our individualistic tendencies toward successful collaboration on larger collective goals. The diverse groups we try to pull more from should be accretive to the military's overall mission.

While there are many categories of difference, what has been proven time and again to be beneficial to success are all the prior mentioned groups of diversity. "Diversity of thought" is a term often thrown around as the final goal of what we're trying to achieve. An extension of this is personality-type diversity and experiences-had diversity. While these are great categories that may enable growth for organizations that can identify blind spots, there is less available data showing their impact and ability to drive better success outcomes. For now, we'll focus mainly on the traditional categories of racial, sexual identity, and cultural diversity, which has yielded significant proven gains for organizations that have focused on them. This is especially true since minority groups in these categories have often been previously excluded from participation entirely. We can't allow for the easy cop-out of claiming diversity by just picking and choosing representative niche categories that fit what our current organizations have. We must actively seek out diversity in the groups that are least represented but have large recruiting pools with a lot to offer. This is the most challenging task to do. An organization like the military is ultimately cut from many different cloths but wears the same unifying one to work every day.

Gen Z's individualism and dealing with diverse changes are really a story of majorities moving to pluralities. Once we recognize this, there will be less fear among extremists on both sides. On the racial front particularly, while the biggest group of Gen-Z Americans are still white, they are slowly becoming a plurality rather than the majority. This doesn't mean that white people should run from fear due to what's been described as the "browning of America." It just means that white kids today will have more peers of different races. On the flip side, while growth in other races is a great boon to America, this shouldn't lead to minority groups failing to recognize that millions of White Americans still comprise the largest racial group and are not hell-bent on oppressing others. We must move the conversation from animosity to coexistence, and then even further to collaboration and co-creation so that together we are producing the strongest force possible.

From a Z demographic perspective, the Latino population, in particular, has grown in large numbers in recent years, making them the largest minority group in the United States. Gen Z also witnessed firsthand the #BlackLivesMatter protests that saw black Americans push for various reforms and a call to be recognized and heard. On the sexual identity front, a recent Gallup poll found that around 20% of Gen Zers identify as lesbian, gay, bisexual, transgender, or queer.[138] As a first step, Z wants to be seen for their differences. They want that difference noticed rather than hidden like in the past. From the actual military data, this mosaic of differences is usually painted positively compared to other high-functioning societal organizations. As a generalization of all service branches, the numbers reflect a slightly more diverse group than the general population. In all armed services, racial minority representation is higher among females than males.[139] The military is forward-leaning in this topic, which Zers want to see and appreciate when attention is drawn to this.

The previously mentioned step one of seeing the difference when it comes to diversity is the easy part. The difference has been seen for decades. The change nowadays is that that difference is being measured and counted. People are actually statistically and scientifically using numbers and data to pay attention to the differences they're seeing. These identities that Z holds and wants to be seen for are one thing, but step two of DEI is understanding the difference. To use a math analogy, equity is really the first derivative of diversity. It's not enough to see the difference among Zers; one has to understand the difference in a way that allows the clarity of fairness. Understanding the difference encompasses conversations and study that enable others to gain insight into the unique struggles, mindsets, and skill sets that different groups may bring to the table.

Take the famous Navajo code talkers of WWII. Savvy military planners realized that these native American military members spoke a unique language that the Japanese couldn't understand. They then employed them to create unbreakable codes. This was an understanding of diverse differences that led to great military gain. It also promoted equity and fairness as these code talkers were treated with great respect and served with distinction. Equity, as we often say in America, is about equality of opportunity, not equality of outcome. We can promote fair opportunities when we begin to see, account for, and document cultural differences. The military's unique meritocracy, where everyone starts out getting yelled at equally in boot camp, is the perfect example. All different cultures, races, and identities are thrown together in one very challenging experience and forced to work together to succeed. The initial entry-level military experience alone is perhaps the most successful equity example in the entire country. This should be presented to Z to emphasize the genuinely equitable environment that entry-level training brings.

The final piece toward implementing a workplace that Z desires is inclusion, which is really a demand of accepting that difference. While internal sentiment and viewpoint are invariably what we care most about, external world polling may give strong insight into what's currently broken with our systems. Pew surveyed 16 other nations about their views regarding America. We ranked highest in entertainment, technological innovation, and our military. A powerful 6 in 10 believe our military to be the strongest or one of the strongest. International Zers say our universities are the best around but also believe that discrimination is a prominent issue in the US: Around 40% call discrimination a very serious problem,[140] It's not enough to just see and understand differences. As a society, we must go further to accept those differences and then implement them toward actionable results. In the broadest sense, inclusion is feeling valued for one's differences at work.

While every military member may wear a matching uniform, the identities they conceal under that uniform matter deeply to Zers. Diversity and equity are about getting different groups of people into the proverbial "command tent" so they have a seat where decisions are made. What's meant explicitly by accepting via inclusion is that the unique perspective you bring to said command tent is felt welcomed inside that tent. You aren't just pushed off to the side because you fill some random DoD directive on DEI; instead, you are included in the discussion, and your thoughts matter.

From the highest echelons to the lowest, this issue will continue to matter to Z. Professor Stephanie Creary, a leading researcher in the field, writes, "Many newer and younger employees are passionate about DEI work and are looking for opportunities to help their companies. One option would be to create DEI sponsor roles for non-managerial employees."[141] Just like how collateral billets exist within units for substance abuse counseling and voting representation, an inclusion billet would be an excellent opportunity for young Zers themselves to work with commanders on issues regarding workplace inclusivity. If given to some of the junior members of the unit, it would be an opportunity to tighten the feedback loop between the Z generation and their elders on an issue that Z cares about.

The beautiful thing about our institution is that at the end of the day a rifle is a rifle, and the people to your left and right are the only thing you can rely on to save your own life. We look out for each other better and on a deeper level than anywhere else in society, no matter what background we are. We break normal societal bonds and accept each other's differences. Ask any former service member about their time in the military and they will tell you the same thing: the people next to them are why they fought and why they succeeded. I remember my first day in the military as I looked around and saw faces, heard accents, and watched interactions between legitimately every group that America has to offer. A few months later all that difference was melded into a combat-trained fighting force that was stronger than anything the world has ever seen. The reason that the US military is the most powerful force ever assembled isn't our superior technology or amazing training, it's our diverse people from our diverse nation.

DEI is an acronym that isn't going away. For many generation Zers, the desire to promote and see diversity, equity, and inclusion in the workplace is a driving force when making career decisions. Even if groups continue to argue and disagree over what it means and to what extent it matters, seeing each other's differences, understanding them, and accepting them will make any organization smarter. Doing those three things is, at its core, the American way and something that the military has excelled at. The messaging to Z regarding these issues should be two-fold. Firstly, the military is one of the most meritocratic and best societal organizations concerning the past history and current policy on diversity initiatives. Second, the military still has work to do in this category and needs young Zers to help work on this. No other private-sector organization is as big or impactful as the military regarding this issue. Empowering Zoomers with initiatives like becoming unit DEI sponsors is one way to appeal to their desire for agency in bettering this initiative. On the more macro front, the military should look to remarket this work into seeing, understanding, and accepting difference.

It's become so inflammatory nowadays when DEI is mentioned that groups on either side of the political, social, or fill-in-the-blank spectrum will seize on it in a fury. The military exists to defend freedom. To do that, it wants and needs the best people of this nation to perform in the highest-functioning teams possible. Recognizing, understanding, and accepting each other's differences isn't some "woke" social experiment; instead, it's the best way forward. At the same time, pushing personal agendas to the detriment of group success just to hit some unhinged-from-reality numerical metric is also highly detrimental.

Some suggestions to solve this issue include putting recruiting stations in places that have historically low enlistment rates. Other suggestions include creating specific marketing branded to attract different demographics. While there may be merit in tactical solutions like those, the more sustainable, higher-level solution comes from military leaders speaking publicly and openly about this issue. Silence is often the go-to when it comes to highly charged discussions around this.

The debate has been made evident in the heated exchanges between Chairmen of the Joint Chiefs and Congress on various books they were reading. Beliefs on controversial topics like this that divide the country are missing the point.

A more important focus should be on the military policy of talking publicly about issues. Lieutenant General Donohue of the 82nd Airborne Division was investigated for a public tweet. Donohue made an innocuous reply to a news anchor after defending a reenlistment ceremony he did for a female soldier.[142] Donohue leaned in and spoke up when the act was attacked online. He didn't sit back; instead, he defended one of his own and showed that the military would honor and accept differences. It's examples like this where senior leaders protect all those in uniform regardless of class, color, or creed. However, the policy of suspending Donohue because he defended his diversity stance doesn't encourage other leaders to speak up. The organization Z wants to join is one that allows for apolitical public discussion and non-biased commentary on the topic of diversity. That is the type of different organization the Armed Services must become.

While a more diverse military makes it stronger, there is a major problem looming on the horizon. The environment is in such a poor state that if we don't address this ecological disaster, we may not be ready for our next major fight. The next chapter discusses how the military can be the prime protector of the environment that Gen Z cares so much about.

CHAPTER 20:
Healing the Environment with the World's Greatest Team

A s hard as it has been to classify and analyze the entirety of Gen Z, there is one unifying issue that nearly all Zers agree on. Primarily due to the existential threat it poses to their future, this issue is literally a matter of survival. Climate change and the environment's health are consistently ranked as some of the Zoomers' top concerns. Z has grown up in a time where the majority consensus in America now strongly recognizes the need to save the planet. While there may be an ongoing debate about the immediacy of the issue and the proper ways to address it, the overwhelming view in Z is to help heal the earth. The mobilization efforts, protests, and even career choices that many Zers are making to deal with this should be seen as a predictive signal about the future.

The military has been equally adamant about climate concerns since the beginning of the 21st century. A recent DoD report cites how a poorer environmental forecast could challenge the various humanitarian operations we provide worldwide. The issues aren't just foreign, they affect the homeland as well. Many older Zers witnessed American troops deploy domestically to deal with the aftermath of Hurricane Katrina. The effect of climate change will see the closing down of training exercises due to fire hazards, flooding hurting naval port readiness, and a hotter world with food/water scarcity leading to higher chances of conflict.[143] Climate problems need to be dealt with by everyone, and Z is watching closely how various organizations respond. Whoever is seen as spearheading the effort to combat climate change will win the recruiting race among generation Z. Luckily, if there is one organization best equipped to organize and fight massive problems, it is the United States military. The environment is making us weaker, harming our ability to fight, and will end up killing us if something isn't done. We need to signal that the military cares deeply about our generation's most important issue.

Sustainability is the big word used by Zers today. Zers care about building a sustainable future so that they can live better than or at least at the level of their parents. There is immense fear[144] about the state of the environment to the point that some Zers in the U.S. are refusing to have children for fear of what the world may become.[145] COVID caused the most significant drop in childbirth since the all-volunteer force was established, and the numbers have only slightly recovered from there. Gen Z will likely facilitate a continued decrease in American birth rates, and climate change may be one key driver. Protecting the earth is the one known, immediate fight that will be decided by Gen Z and will undoubt-edly impact their grandchildren if they ever have them. The seriousness of the environmental issue is also being noticed in polling.

The message has been spread so far and in such daunting ways that around 70% of surveyed Zers actually report anxiety when seeing a climate-related post online.[146] While the movement has seen youth activists like Greta Thunberg skyrocket to fame, the average Zer isn't yet picketing their local government office. The critical point here is that for Z, there may be lots of disagreement on society and the future, but there is agreement that we don't want to live on a more polluted earth. We don't want to need gas masks to go outside or to no longer visit some American cities because they are submerged underwater. These aren't controversial or striking claims. Every one of all age groups likely subconsciously understands what is at stake here. However, Z uniquely realizes the issue for two primary reasons.

Firstly, by being young, they have the most to lose. We have yet to get the prime periods of our lives in and would like to do so on a hospitable planet. Secondly, we have been taught from a young age about the issue. When "going green" was seen as a fringe idea, it wasn't talked about nearly as much in schools for millennials. Now, it's safe to bet that nearly every Zer had at least one lesson on the environment growing up. They've been taught early on that only by taking individual action like recycling, together we can combat this ultimate free-rider issue. For Z, saving the environment has become personal, and it has created a newfound unity around the cause.

Climate policy will continue to be a major factor when Z chooses jobs. Private sector companies have caught onto the trend and are now vehemently displaying their "climate scorecards" to attract new employ-ees. They understand that the longer-term view here is what is going to win. Take Italian fashion brand Cucinelli, which caps its profits to give back to its workers and the environment and promote long-term, sustainable growth.[147] They've realized that what was once known as the "i-generation" is really more like the "we generation" in that it will take a good majority of Z's efforts to tilt the planetary trend back on track. The US Army famously had Uncle Sam screaming, "I want you," in order to convince people to join. The most effective pitch today would probably have the earth saying, "I need you," with a company emblem in the background.

LinkedIn, the largest online network for job seekers, released their "Global Green Skills Report," showing an astounding number of future jobs requiring some level of environmentally-focused skills.[148] Employers not only need people thinking about the earth, they also recognize that to attract Z, they need to demonstrate their eco-friendly prowess. This dual-sided dance will likely continue into an all-out enviro-arms race that sees companies trying to outdo each other to prove who cares more. Perhaps some of this is futile posturing, but Z will note those who fail to participate altogether. The firms with the most Z recruiting success will have some ability to message their environmental impact to the generation.

Many believe that wars are won primarily with armies and weapons. In reality, mother nature is often a key decider on the battlefield. Climate, geography, and weather, in particular, have impacted every major conflict in history. Napoleon's conquest of Russia was famously stopped because of a harsh winter and an even harsher and less-talked-about summer. Weather will only continue to have an even more outsized effect in the wars of the future. Since the nature of war always involves nature itself, the military is in a prime position to demonstrate how important this issue is. Very few other industries and businesses are as directly impacted by climate as defense is. Although the organization at large and our leaders care deeply about this issue, the current disconnect is that Z and society doesn't automatically associate the military with the environment. There's a signaling and branding gap here since most civilians think battle relates to human vs. human actions. If the military can successfully show just how impacted by the environment we are, as well as how positively impactful to the environment we can be, we will begin to turn the tide.

No other entity in the world is as impacted by climate change, nor has the means to metaphorically move the temperature down a few degrees. The impact of the armed forces is worldwide, encountering every natural episode possible and offering a first-hand seat in battling the danger headed our way. Due to this, society must begin associating the role of defeating climate change with the DoD. While many organizations will have to participate in the fight, the primary defender of us all should be the one to lead on this problem. While there are some great volunteer organizations like Americorps, and new proposals include creating a climate corps like the Peace Corps, the military should be the one to assume the climate role to enlist eager Z volunteers. The military must be presented as the greatest force in solving climate change to capitalize on the huge rush of Zers who see it as their destiny to participate in these issues. At first, it may seem odd or misplaced that a warfighting organization is a place to go to "green" the planet and heal the earth. However, the moment that pictures of horrible hurricanes and towering tsunamis are splashed on screens, and the average person runs in fear, it's often DoD first responders who go into harm's way and save lives.

Instead, the job of protecting and defending the way we live is the marketing message that needs to be sent out. The DoD can satisfy all Gen Z's environmentalist needs by placing that person in the best position to impact the environment. With more money and research projects than any other federal agency, it's the armed services where a new recruit can access the most programs and tools. Indeed, there won't be much time for tree planting or oil spill clean-up in the first training iterations. However, sending the message to Z that they can be the new voices in the force responsible for tackling these problems will have great appeal. The skills they'll learn in the military and the ability to solve complex problems in a team are exactly what they'll need to rescue the planet. These recruits will hopefully rise to eventually set policy. On duty, they can have an outsized impact on units as they advise how each group can be more green-conscious. Little things like not throwing personal hygiene trash or spent ammunition casings into the woods will make a real difference. This bottom-up approach will impact more environmental levers due to the size of the military than any other corporation or work activity.

It's interesting to imagine what future military jobs will arise to combat climate change. It's likely too early to begin creating climate-specific career fields or starting to stand up environmental battalions within each service branch. Military weather analysts exist in the uniformed services, but it will likely be a few years until something like an "environmental emissions specialist" is formed. Still, the military conducts numerous humanitarian aid missions annually, and it would be wise to begin branding them as environmental rescue operations. As radical as it sounds, it's possible shortly that the military will be tasked to take steps to prevent environmental catastrophes. Perhaps destroying harmful emitter sites and securing eco-friendly complexes across the globe will someday become missions. Defense officials must then shape the perception by better highlighting what is already occurring and what is planned for the future. For now, the messaging has to be clear to a generation concerned with the world's health: the best way to make a difference in the environment is by joining the military.

While the environment is the long-term dilemma on the horizon, in the near-term there is a more ominous threat headed our way. The next chapter examines our near-peer competitor and its impact on recruiting.

CHAPTER 21:

Preparing for the Next Big War

The time has come to be bluntly honest about our current situation. This recruiting crisis shows that America's all-volunteer force cannot continue to operate successfully if some change doesn't occur. We may not feel we are at war now, so nobody cares, but we are already fighting a battle. Our largest competitor, China, threatens us more every day. On February 2nd, 2023, it was announced that a Chinese spy balloon was flying over the continental US.[149] While the instant hysteria this caused in the media wasn't as pronounced as the Sputnik moment with the Soviets, it created enough fear to get the public thinking. Some began to wonder what would happen if thousands of these balloons appeared

WE DON'T WANT YOU, UNCLE SAM

over our cities one day...potentially carrying lethal munitions. Instead, the better question concerns the current manpower shortages we face. The military is ready to defend the U.S. homeland if and only if it has the necessary troops to do so. Most young Zers and probably Americans, in general, believe a war scenario involving the US homeland is ludicrous. Unfortunately, this thinking is dangerous for a superpower like America. The United Kingdom, an empire the sun never set on, was surprise-attacked by Nazi Germany in WWII. Luckily, its citizens sprang into action and thankfully had enough fighter pilots to defend the skies of London. China vs. us already presents a brutal equation when it comes to numbers. A tragic attack like 9/11 shouldn't be the wake-up call needed that encourages Zers to serve.

We all must have the conversation that if we want to continue living as a free nation with overseas interests, then we must do something to change what is currently occurring. This isn't intended to sound overly alarmist or dramatic; instead, it is simply the cold, hard truth. The time to prepare for battle is now, in the early stages of the conflict, so we can decisively deter kinetic combat or quickly end it once it starts. However, we won't have a fighting chance in a major foreign war if we don't have anyone here ready to fight. We may have all the advanced weaponry and the latest technology our great innovators have to offer, but without warfighters, it is useless. We're facing a more powerful and larger threat than anything we've dealt with in decades. That should scare the living Sierra Hotel India Tango out of every American. As an intelligence professional not at liberty to discuss any classified material or daily workings, I can tell you that my private thoughts are enough to cause terror in the minds of an average U.S. person.

It is now up to the media and citizens to properly report and portray how intensely we are already competing. One of the leading advocates for modernizing the DoD's technology and systems is Christian Brose. His book *The Kill Chain* explains how we are falling behind in the procurement race as he remarks, "We convinced ourselves that the period of peace and prosperity we were enjoying was uniquely the result of our virtues, our values, and our power, and that all of it would last forever."[150] That forever is ending now. It's equally up to the media and our citizenry to promote service and encourage Zers to give to the nation's forces. From a cultural perception standpoint, Z doesn't want to serve if the government, but more so, society doesn't want to give back to them. Suppose it's continuously perceived that the American public doesn't live up to its obligations to those who make sacrifices. In that case, anything we try will ultimately fail to reverse the numerical downtrend. For reference, when it comes to numbers, we have a smaller military today than we did ten years ago, which was smaller than it was 20 years ago but still smaller than it was 30 years ago. The WWII parades may be a thing of the past, but back then when we asked our young people, who were mostly average and regular, to do extraordinary and incredible things...they stepped up. The small group of people doing those things now are equally incredible and should be respected as such.

Unfortunately, the pressure on service isn't just coming from this new external threat. We're actually fighting an equally painful influence war internally against ourselves. The election meddling, spying, and foreign government interference in our domestic affairs pale in comparison to the perception battle being pitched at home. Our collective goal must be to make national service the desired norm among Zers. One of the most popular apps that Gen Zers use nowadays is Chinese-owned Tik Tok. While certain laws have banned Tik Tok on military bases, the collection capabilities the app provides the People's Republic of China are immense. Even further, their algorithms' influence power is strong enough to hold massive sway over Z. They can potentially persuade Zers away from military service, while also stoking domestic strife in our nation. Even if we ascribe that the CCP successfully censors and brainwashes its citizens, we must be wary of what apps like these can subconsciously do to our own citizens. The real battlefield where the China-U.S. conflict is taking place is in the minds of our free-thinking populace.

Whether we like it or not, the Communist party enjoys broad support from its Z-aged population. Chinese Zers are nationalistic and ready to fight: "Many Chinese youth feel a genuine sense of triumphalist, resolute pride in their country. Some of them may view the country's rise as both empirically inevitable (as a means of thwarting the West-led global order)."[151] In our nation, we currently stand divided. The media has a huge job and national security responsibility to play here as we head down what could end up being a bloody road. A poignant example is when the Twitter files exposed that the Pentagon was trying similar social-media influence tactics. One American media writer, Lee Fang, titled his article "Twitter Aided the Pentagon in Its Covert Online Propaganda Campaign."[152] The instantly negative Pentagon bashing will not help shape American Z's perceptions of the military. Ironically, there's not an equally negative article bashing the Chinese Communist use of social media for propaganda. The public opinion domain is now like land, air, and sea. Information is a full part of warfare, and in information, we aren't just losing...we're getting slaughtered.

All hope isn't lost in this perception struggle. Society needs to realize that the threat is here and must work together to push Z into desiring time in service. With all the government and military bashing present in many sectors of society, the most powerful military force assembled still incites respect and has a weight to it unlike any other. I used to give info sessions for prospective Wharton students. A slide listed about 100 of the most influential company logos that our graduates work at. On it, the DoD's logo of the eagle carrying arrows still garnered a higher level of respect from those in the audience. Everyday citizens are still deeply impacted by thinking about national defense when it is presented directly to them…when it is put right in front of their eyes. One proposal as we try to promote a newfound surge in service deals with blending the more traditional citizen-soldier concept that helped found our country.

Many Zers would willingly work with the DoD and support our national security if they could do so without fully entering the active duty all-volunteer force. Initiatives like GigEagle from the Defense Innovation Unit that one day aims to match reserve and civilian skill sets with short-term gig work for the DoD are an excellent place to start. If more people get tangentially connected to the military, the exposure will naturally lead to higher recruitment. The prospect of renting skills from the civilian populace holds some merit. Rather than having an extremely large continuous standing force that takes time and money, an augmentation reserve that can rotate in and out of public and private service may be a model as we advance. This would also help with retention. Most of those in service look at their transition off of active-duty as a hard, all-or-nothing break point, but allowing for some to remain connected in a civilian or semi-reserve capacity would retain key abilities. Regardless of the overall mechanism, that "propensity" to at least be in some way involved in defense needs to be continuously fostered and rejuvenated in Z.

In the end, the current status quo is not sustainable. Many academics, military strategists, and politicians seem lost as to what to do. Short of a formalized military draft like back in Vietnam, some worry that we'll never be able to hit the necessary numbers. Without even speculating what a modern 21st-century draft would look like, it's hard to imagine the societal commotion and outcry that it would cause. In my assessment, there is just enough time left, a quickly fleeting window, to successfully save the all-volunteer force concept and cure the military recruitment crisis if we band together in a new push for national service. Recently, a growing chorus of thinkers has started promoting this idea. Richard Hass, president of the Council on Foreign Relations, writes, "Why should we want young Americans to perform one or two years of government service? One reason is that a common experience would help break down some of the barriers that have arisen owing to geography, class, race, religion, education, language, and more."[153] The issue is that there are currently many different flavors of what this would look like, and broadening the scope of it too widely risks clouding its impact.

Our first and most immediate push for national service should focus on defense, specifically manning the armed forces with generation Z recruits so that our military can defend the United States in the wars to come. The cornerstone of the push towards reinvigorating a sense of national service involves changing the norm. Right now, the norm is not to serve society but to go out individually and secure a job. The most desirable places to work don't have recruiting issues. Frequently these are technology and finance jobs, the ones that pay the most. A few institutions buck this trend, and it would be interesting to model them. Capitol Hill employs thousands of young staffers who end up being the driving force behind making Congress work. This government work is extremely underpaid and involves long hours with challenging tasks, yet it never seems to lack applicants. In fact, it's actually extremely competitive to get a job on the Hill. The underlying reason is that Hill work gives staffers agency, the ability to feel as though they have an impact, and sets them up amazingly for success with future connections and credibility. The military must become this type of place for Z. We must make it a place that doesn't have a recruiting deficit but rather a surplus. We may never succeed in making the military the most desirable workplace, but we need to make it an experience people desire.

The calls are growing for initiatives like a "service year" with a mandated effort that would act as a rite of passage between high school and the "adult world." Efforts that push to get the population working together are excellent as they lead to the concept of a physical social network to connect and solve our societal problems. However, of paramount importance is that we focus first and foremost on filling key military shortfalls. The traditional sense of service to the nation in the armed forces can't be by a modernist approach to enriching communities and our social fabric. I firmly believe that through more military participation, we can do those things well, but due to the current state of our world, defense rings primary, or we won't have anything left to enrich because it will have been so destroyed in war. A dark night is approaching fast. Will anyone be there to man the wall?

America has long been seen as the bastion of freedom, as the provider of individual liberties to the rest of the world. A nation that started as a mere experiment has more than made its mark on human history. Today we are at a basic crossroads among our own domestic populace. Never before have young Americans experienced such freedom, but never before have those same Americans been needed as much to provide that level of Freedom to their country and the rest of the world. The concept of service in itself denotes an inherently voluntary nature to it. Making it so socially desirable to dedicate time to national service has to be the preferred route forward. Apart from everything discussed already, the truly only way to do this is to make service part of the normal conversation of youth development in the U.S. In schools, on television, with employers, between friends, at the dinner table, and eventually with oneself, a massive push to discuss military service will be what puts this idea at the forefront of every Zer's mind.

If Generation Z were successfully induced to have the propensity to serve, then one day, nobody would have to say, "Thank you for your service." This would instead change to "Thank you for letting me serve." In future history, it would be said that the generation of Americans that took on the greatest experiment since our founding would be deemed to be the ones that saved us all. Perhaps Z stands for Zero. In binary, Zeros make up part of computer code, and Zero to One is the concept of innovating to get over the very large initial starting hurdle. Generation Zero has a nice ring to it, the generation that began a new Pax Americana.

CONCLUSION:

Answering the Call of Duty

In the end, it is up to the young Americans themselves, who comprise generation Z, to make a decision about serving in the military. Will they take command and be leaders for our country? Will they step up when we need people and answer the Call of Duty like so many before them? For me, leading Marines while serving this nation has been the greatest experience of my life. More than anything else I've ever done, the connections I've made with those serving next to me have provided life-changing value.

Around 85 years ago, researchers at Harvard began what is currently considered one of the longest ongoing research projects. They started by tracking 270 people on various metrics throughout their lives. The work gives powerful, time-tested insight into many of life's biggest questions. Perhaps most striking is the conclusion that "Close relationships, more

than money or fame, are what keep people happy throughout their lives...
Those ties protect people from life's discontents, help to delay mental
and physical decline, and are better predictors of long and happy lives
than social class, I.Q., or even genes.[154]" Tying this in with the analysis of
Sebastian Junger, the famed author of *War* and *Tribe,* shows a common
thread. When explaining why a combat vet heavily missed war, Junger
remarks, "He missed, in some ways, the opposite of killing. What he
missed was the connection to the other men he was with."[155] If it is the
relationships we make in life that matter most for our well-being, and
the military uniquely offers some of the deepest and most connected
relationships possible, then a clear value proposition for military service
begins to reveal itself.

The true thesis of this writing was that: through the use of personal
life stories and macro analysis, this book explains why military recruiting
in the United States is at an all-time low to suggest ways that American
society and its leaders can fix this issue. Part 1 provided a baseline of who
Generation Z is and how we think. It explained that in order to solve the
recruiting crisis, we have to first grasp just how different Z is compared
to past age cohorts. Part 2 discussed key expectations that Gen Z has for
the modern workplace. It explained some improvements the military can
make in its day-to-day administration to better appeal to Zoomers. Part
3 talked about various cultural factors impacting young America, and
provided guidance on how to interpret them in the context of recruiting
the new force. Finally, Part 4 showed how the military can impact larger
society and be used for good in our country and world.

We must rebuild the notion of military service by demonstrating the
benefits of the world's greatest physical social network. After analyzing the
unique issues the military faces with recruiting generation Z, it's clear that
the single most important message leaders can emphasize about service are

the ties you gain during your time in duty. By serving, American youths enrich their bonds with themselves, other people, and society in ways that no other activity or job will ever come close to matching.

This physical social network that I am trying to explain is a multi-faceted concept, one that, by nature, is nebulous and hard to define. In essence, it provides all the benefits, innovation, and connections of a digital social network, but it does so in reality. Real people making real relationships for life in the real, physical world. Silicon Valley has given America's youth a work environment it can aspire to. While these companies themselves may currently be at their own inflection points, the networks they provided their employees were unlike anywhere else in the US. Forget all the cushy office perks and lenient vacation policies, tech companies brought together some of the smartest kids in America and gave them a place where they actually wanted to work. A place they aspired to join above all else. A job at Google, no matter what function, was once seen as the highest of highs. Applicants were turned away in droves for the few spots that existed to enter this heavenly community. While there have been whole books written about how Silicon Valley and the military need to work together more to create the best technology and develop cutting-edge systems to defend us, the real innovation they should be giving the military is their human resource practices. Imagine if the military became as desirable to join as a large tech company?

Ray Dalio, the founder of the world's largest hedge fund, writes,"[156] "The essential difference between a culture of people with shared values and a cult is the extent to which there is independent thinking. Cults demand unquestioning obedience. Thinking for yourself and challenging others' ideas is anti-cult behavior.". The military should promote independent thinking based on shared values... which is the true essence of what I mean by a physical social network. The military can provide the answer to what so many young people are looking for like it has in the past, and it should change so that it can continue to provide it in the future by attracting new recruits.

As I wrap up my year-long study of this issue, I want to tell you, the reader, that I am actually hopeful about us coming together to solve this problem. One of the most important things I read over this time was about a young boy who served in the Continental Army at just fourteen years old. As our country struggled for its founding, he rose up in the common defense and guarded meat and food for our soldiers. In a full-scale revolution in the face of a foreign invader, the first generation of Americans banded together to fight. While very different and hundreds of years separated from Generation Z, that founding generation leaves us much to aspire to. That young boy risked everything to protect his family, his future children, and the cause he believed in.

The experience as a servicemember clearly shaped his worldview when he went on to lead a successful private life as a meat packer in upstate New York. He relied on his familiarity with the things he learned in the military and worked to contribute to the local economy. He even went so far as dedicating time to public civic life. This new citizen was a model for others, relying on bonds with family, friends, and acquaintances to flourish. He developed along with his fledgling nation but when the British returned in 1812, he once again stepped up to serve it. During that war he was too old to fight and instead helped supply much-needed meat to our troops. When those Soldiers received that food, they saw this man's unique labeling on his barrels with the letters "U.S." Legend developed from there that this man, Samuel Wilson, was given the nickname that will go down in history as "Uncle Sam."

The reason this little-known tale resonates so much is that it is not hard to imagine that, in our country today, there exist hundreds of thousands of people just like this. Individual citizens from all corners of America wandering down various paths just waiting for the boost that joining the military would give them. Each of them standing by for their story to be written down in history and for some organization to give them the impact they need to reach their full potential. By deeply analyzing that organization and then prescribing various changes, we can show generation Z that what many are searching for is right in front of us.

Perhaps there comes a time when there is no need for nations to go to war against one another. When the entire world is united in fighting some intergalactic alien invader like in many sci-fi series and novels. Perhaps that invader is already here with the onset of Chat GPT, Bard, and artificial intelligence. Even then, the world will need a military, and the young citizens of earth will have to be recruited to successfully defend our planet. From ancient history to the distant future, military recruiting will remain an essential topic that should be studied and debated. May the coming night be less dark than it currently appears, and may we collectively see through it with the right vision. Only by working together in a united way can we make it so that one day Generation Z says, "We Want You, Uncle Sam"!

Please feel free to comment with your thoughts and ideas for solving the recruitment crisis on www.unclesambook.org

About the Author

Second Lieutenant Matthew Weiss is a Signals Intelligence/Electronic Warfare Officer in the United States Marine Corps. Previously, he worked in mergers and acquisitions at a cutting-edge defense technology company. He holds a BS and an MBA from the Wharton School at the University of Pennsylvania. Most importantly, he is a member of Generation Z who cares deeply about solving this issue of service.

Endnotes

1   Tiron, Roxana. "US Military Faces Biggest Recruiting Hurdles in 50 Years (1)." Bloomberg Government, September 21, 2022. https://about.bgov.com/news/us-military-services-face-biggest-recruiting-hurdles-in-50-years/.

2   Bloomberg, Michael R. "US Military Has a Recruitment and Retention Problem. Here's How to Fix It." Bloomberg.com. Bloomberg, August 8, 2022.https://www.bloomberg.com/opinion/articles/2022-08-08/us-military-has-a-recruitment-and-retention-problem-here-s-how-to-fix-it.

3   Gehlhaus, Diana, Youth Information Networks and Propensity to Serve in the Military. Santa Monica, CA: RAND Corporation, 2021. https://www.rand.org/pubs/rgs_dissertations/RGSDA1662-1.html.

4   Armed Services Subcommittee on Personnel. Testimony. "Status of Military Recruiting" (117 AD).

5   Dimock, Michael. "Defining Generations: Where Millennials End and Generation Z Begins." Pew Research Center. Pew Research Center, April 21, 2022. https://www.pewresearch.org/fact-tank/2019/01/17/where-millennials-end-and-generation-z-begins/.

6   Rep. *Reagan National Defense Survey* , 2022.

7   Wrzesniewski, Amy, Clark McCauley, Paul Rozin, and Barry Schwartz. "Jobs, Careers, and Callings: People's Relations to Their Work." *Journal of Research in Personality* 31, no. 1 (1997): 21–33. https://doi.org/10.1006/jrpe.1997.2162.

8   Gulati, Ranjay. "The Great Resignation or the Great Rethink?" Harvard Business Review, March 25, 2022. https://hbr.org/2022/03/the-great-resignation-or-the-great-rethink.

9   De Witte, Melissa. "What to Know about Gen Z." Stanford News, January 3, 2022. https://news.stanford.edu/2022/01/03/know-gen-z/.

10   Michas, Frederic. "Total Active Physicians in the U.S. 2022, by State," 2022. https://www.statista.com/statistics/186269/total-active-physicians-in-the-us/

11   Gianfagna, Mike. "What Is Moore's Law?: Is Moore's Law Dead?" Synopsys. Synopsys, June 30, 2021. https://www.synopsys.com/glossary/what-is-moores-law.html#:~:text=Definition,as%20E%20%3D%20mc2).

12   Cravo, André Mascioli, Gustavo Brito de Azevedo, Cristiano Moraes Bilacchi Azarias, Louise Catheryne Barne, Fernanda Dantas Bueno, Raphael Y. de Camargo, Vanessa Carneiro Morita, et al. "Time Experience during Social Distancing: A Longitudinal Study during the First Months of Covid-19 Pandemic in Brazil." *Science Advances* 8, no. 15 (2022). https://doi.org/10.1126/sciadv.abj7205.

13   Elmore, Tim, and Andrew McPeak. *Generation Z Unfiltered: Facing Nine Hidden Challenges of the Most Anxious Population*. Atlanta, GA: Poet Gardener Publishing in association with Growing Leaders, Inc., 2019.

14   Kirkcaldy, Bruce D., Roy J. Shephard, and Adrian F. Furnham. "The Influence of Type a Behaviour and Locus of Control upon Job Satisfaction and Occupational Health." *Personality and Individual Differences* 33, no. 8 (2002): 1361–71. https://doi.org/10.1016/s0191-8869(02)00018-1.

15   Rep. *American Opportunity Survey*. McKinsey, 2022.

16   Christensen, Clayton M. 2012. *How Will You Measure Your Life?* London, England: HarperCollins.

17   Busch, Judith W. "Mentoring in Graduate Schools of Education: Mentors' Perceptions." *American Educational Research Journal* 22, no. 2 (1985): 257–65. https://doi.org/10.3102/00028312022002257.

18   Stillman, Jonah. *Gen Z @ Work - How The Next Generation Is Transforming the Workplace*. HarperCollins Publishers Inc, 2017.

19   Halevy, Nir, Eileen Y. Chou, and Adam D. Galinsky. "A Functional Model of Hierarchy." *Organizational Psychology Review* 1, no. 1 (2011): 32–52. https://doi.org/10.1177/2041386610380991.

20   Lindenfors, Johan Lind and Patrik. "Why We Dispute 'Dunbar's Number': Can People Really Maintain Only 150 Relationships?" Phys.org. Phys.org, June 23, 2021. https://phys.org/news/2021-06-dispute-dunbar-people-relationships. html.

21   Ed, Carnegie Higher. "What Makes Gen Z Click: 5 Defining Differences between Gen Z and Millennials: Carnegie-Higher Ed." Carnegie, February 7, 2022. https://www.carnegiehighered.com/blog/ what-makes-gen-z-click-5-defining-differences-between-gen-z-and-millen- nials/#:~:text=Unlike%20their%20millennial%20counterparts%2C%20 Gen,including%20acceptance%20at%20your%20university.

22   Steinhenge, Anna, Dan Cable, and Duncan Wardley. "The Pros and Cons of Competition among Employees." Harvard Business Review, July 25, 2017. https://hbr.org/2017/03/the-pros-and-cons-of-competition-among-employ- ees#:~:text=Some%20research%20studies%20suggest%20such,effort%20 and%20enables%20higher%20performance.

23   Hutmacher, Fabian. "Why Is There So Much More Research on Vision than on Any Other Sensory Modality?" *Frontiers in Psychology* 10 (2019). https://doi. org/10.3389/fpsyg.2019.02246.

24   Fagan, Abigail. "Why We See What We Want to See." *Psychology Today*. Sussex Publishers. Accessed March 24, 2023. https://www.psychologytoday.com/us/ blog/between-cultures/201907/why-we-see-what-we-want-see.

25   Leaser, David. "Do Digital Badges Really Provide Value to Businesses?" IBM Training and Skills Blog, August 2, 2019. https://www.ibm.com/blogs/ ibm-training/do-digital-badges-really-provide-value-to-businesses/.

26   Sarinopoulos, I., D. W. Grupe, K. L. Mackiewicz, J. D. Herrington, M. Lor, E. E. Steege, and J. B. Nitschke. "Uncertainty during Anticipation Modulates Neural Responses to Aversion in Human Insula and Amygdala." *Cerebral Cortex* 20, no. 4 (2009): 929–40. https://doi.org/10.1093/cercor/bhp155.

27   Stewart-Rozema, Jordan, and Christopher Pratts. "International Student Enrollment Statistics: BestColleges." BestColleges. com, October 12, 2022. https://www.bestcolleges.com/research/ international-student-enrollment-statistics/#fn-1.

28   Slater, Daniel. "Executive Insights." Amazon. Korn/Ferry International, 1999. https://aws.amazon.com/executive-insights/content/amazon-two-pizza-team/.

29   Becker, Ernest. *The Denial of Death*. New York: Free Press, 1973.

30 Winston, Kimberly. "Defense Department Expands Its List of Recognized Religions." Religion News Service, April 23, 2017. https://religionnews.com/2017/04/21/defense-department-expands-its-list-of-recognized-religions/.

31 Burge, Ryan. "Gen Z and Religion in 2021." Religion in Public, June 15, 2022. https://religioninpublic.blog/2022/06/15/gen-z-and-religion-in-2021/.

32 McCammon, Sarah, Michael Levitt, and Kathryn Fox. "America's Christian Majority Is Shrinking, and Could Dip below 50% by 2070." NPR. NPR, September 15, 2022. https://www.npr.org/2022/09/15/1123289466/americas-christian-majority-is-shrinking-and-could-dip-below-50-by-2070.

33 Burdette, Amy M., Victor Wang, Glen H. Elder, Terrence D. Hill, and Janel Benson. "Serving God and Country? Religious Involvement and Military Service among Young Adult Men." *Journal for the Scientific Study of Religion* 48, no. 4 (2009): 794–804. https://doi.org/10.1111/j.1468-5906.2009.01481.x.

34 American Survey Center. "More Than a Third of Gen Z Identifies as Religiously Unaffiliated." American Survey Center, January 17, 2019, https://www.americansurveycenter.org/research/generation-z-future-of-faith/#:~:text=More%20Than%20a%20Third%20of%20Gen%20Z%20Identifies%20as%20Religiously%20Unaffiliated&text=It's%20not%20only%20a%20lack,or%20agnostic%20(9%20percent).

35 McKinsey & Company. *The Young and the Restless: Generation Z in America.* McKinsey & Company, April 2019, https://www.mckinsey.com/industries/retail/our-insights/the-young-and-the-restless-generation-z-in-america.

36 Shkolnikova, Svetlana. "Military Recruiting Problems with Social Media." *Stars and Stripes.* September 21, 2022, https://www.stripes.com/theaters/us/2022-09-21/military-recruiting-problems-social-media-7422004.html.

37 Vespa, Jonathan. "The American Community Survey: A Look at the Economic Well-Being of U.S. Households in 2019." *U.S. Census Bureau*, September 2020. Accessed September 28, 2022. https://www.census.gov/library/publications/2020/demo/acs-43.html.

38 Hughes, Sarah. "Mila Kunis attends Marine Corps Ball with Afghanistan veteran." *The Washington Post.* November 21, 2011. Accessed September 28, 2022. https://www.washingtonpost.com/blogs/celebritology/post/mila-kunis-attends-marine-corp-ball-with-afghanistan-veteran/2011/11/21/gIQAggcchN_blog.html.

39   Sung, Morgan. "TikTok-famous 'Island Boys' promote Army recruitment on
      Cameo." *NBC News*, 16 Nov. 2021, https://www.nbcnews.com/pop-culture/
      viral/tiktok-famous-island-boys-promote-army-recruitment-cameo-rcna13347.

40   United States Navy. "Sailor vs." Navy.com, accessed April 8, 2023, https://www.
      navy.com/explore-the-navy/sailor-vs/.

41   Schaeffer, Katherine. "The Changing Face of America's Veteran Population." Pew
      Research Center. Pew Research Center, April 5, 2021. https://www.pewresearch.
      org/fact-tank/2021/04/05/the-changing-face-of-americas-veteran-population/.

42   Igielnik, Ruth. "Key Findings about America's Military Veterans." Pew Research
      Center. Pew Research Center, May 30, 2020. https://www.pewresearch.org/
      fact-tank/2019/11/07/key-findings-about-americas-military-Veterans/.

43   Mitchell, Travis. "The American Veteran Experience and
      the Post-9/11 Generation." Pew Research Center's Social &
      Demographic Trends Project. Pew Research Center, October 1,
      2021. https://www.pewresearch.org/social-trends/2019/09/10/
      the-american-veteran-experience-and-the-post-9-11-generation/.

44   Amidon, Col. Matthew F. "Veterans May Be Key to Solving the US
      Military Recruitment Crisis." Navy Times. Navy Times, August 25, 2022.
      https://www.militarytimes.com/opinion/commentary/2022/08/23/
      veterans-may-be-key-to-solving-the-us-military-recruitment-crisis/.

45   Directorate of Analytics and Performance Optimization - USMC, Impacts of
      Special Duty Assignments § (2019).

46   Arkes, Jeremy; Jesse M. Cunha and Noah Myung. "Performance Based Incentives
      for Military Recruiters: Evidence from the U.S. Navy." Available at http://hdl.
      handle.net/10945/65136

47   Lim, Nelson, Bruce R. Orvis, and Kimberly Curry Hall. *Leveraging Big
      Data Analytics to Improve Military Recruiting*. Santa Monica, CA: RAND
      Corporation, 2019.

48   Porter, Michael. "The Five Competitive Forces That Shape Strategy."
      Harvard Business Review, January 2008. https://hbr.org/2008/01/
      the-five-competitive-forces-that-shape-strategy.

49   Spoehr, Thomas. "Improving America's Long-Term Military Recruiting
      Outlook." The Heritage Foundation, October 2021. https://www.heritage.org/
      defense/report/improving-americas-long-term-military-recruiting-outlook.

50 Huff, Darrel, and Irving Geis. *How to Lie with Statistics*. New York: Norton, 1993.

51 Sweeney, Evan. "DOD Report Blasts MHS Genesis Rollout, Citing Inaccurate Patient Information and Safety Concerns." Fierce Healthcare, May 14, 2018. https://www.fiercehealthcare.com/tech/dod-cerner-mhs-genesis-patient-safety-interoperability-va.

52 Britzky, Haley. "How the Military's New Medical Screening Is Screwing over Army Recruiters." Task & Purpose, September 15, 2022. https://taskandpurpose.com/news/army-military-genesis-medical-screening-recruiting/.

53 James M. Inhofe National Defense Authorization Act for Fiscal Year 2023

54 Desjardins, Jeff. "Why Generation Z Has a Totally Different Approach to Money." World Economic Forum, November 18, 2018. https://www.weforum.org/agenda/2018/11/why-gen-z-is-approaching-money-differently-than-other-generations-95032cb6-6046-4269-a38a-0763bd7909ff/.

55 Deloitte. *Deloitte Global 2022 Gen Z and Millennial Survey*, 2022.

56 Carnevale, Anthony, Artem Gulish, and Kathryn Campbell. "Youth Policy: How Can We Smooth the Rocky Path to Adulthood?" *Georgetown University McCourt School of Public Policy*, 2021.

57 Bushatz, Amy. "2023 Military Pay Raise Will Be the Largest in 20 Years." Military.com, December 23, 2022. https://www.military.com/daily-news/2022/12/07/2023-military-pay-raise-will-be-largest-20-years.html.

58 Hosek, James, Beth J. Asch, Michael G. Mattock, and Troy D. Smith, Military and Civilian Pay Levels, Trends, and Recruit Quality. Santa Monica, CA: RAND Corporation, 2018. https://www.rand.org/pubs/research_reports/RR2396.html.

59 Asch, Beth J., Navigating Current and Emerging Army Recruiting Challenges: What Can Research Tell Us? Santa Monica, CA: RAND Corporation, 2019. https://www.rand.org/pubs/research_reports/RR3107.html.

60 Winkie, Davis. "Performance Bonuses Could Come Soon, Top Enlisted Soldier Says." Army Times. Army Times, August 19, 2022. https://www.armytimes.com/news/your-army/2022/07/13/performance-bonuses-could-come-soon-top-enlisted-soldier-says/.

61 Bureau of Labor Statistics, Employee Tenure Summary §. USDL-22-1894 (2022).

62 Hoff, Madison. "How Gen Z Is Winning the Great Resignation, from Pay Increases to Better Work-Life Balance." Business Insider. Business Insider. Accessed April 10, 2023. https://www.businessinsider.com/gen-z-winning-great-resignation-changing-job-market-2022-6.

63 John T. Warner, "The Effect of the Civilian Economy on Recruiting and Retention," in U.S. Department of Defense, *Report of the Eleventh Quadrennial Review of Military Compensation*, supporting research papers, Part 1, Chapter 2, June 2012

64 Council on Foreign Relations. "Demographics of the U.S. Military.". Accessed April 9, 2023. https://www.cfr.org/backgrounder/demographics-us-military.

65 Watson, Jason M., and David L. Strayer. "Supertaskers: Profiles in Extraordinary Multitasking Ability." *Psychonomic Bulletin & Review* 17, no. 4 (2010): 479–85. https://doi.org/10.3758/pbr.17.4.479.

66 Murray, Carla Tighe, and Adebayo Adedeji, Approaches to changing military compensation § (2020).

67 Roth-Douquet, Kathy, and Frank Schaeffer. *AWOL: The Unexcused Absence of America's Upper Classes from the Military -- and How It Hurts Our Country*. New York: Collins, 2007.

68 "All-in with Chamath, Jason, Sacks & Friedberg." E111: Microsoft to invest $10B in OpenAI, generative AI hype, America's over-classification problem, 2023. https://allinchamathjason.libsyn.com/e111-microsoft-to-invest-10b-in-openai-generative-ai-hype-americas-over-classification-problem.

69 Fernandez-Araoz, Claudio. "The Rise of the 'Corporate Nomad.'" *Harvard Business Review*, March 30, 2022. https://hbr.org/2022/03/the-rise-of-the-corporate-nomad.

70 Delbert, Caroline. "Jeff Bezos Is Paying for a Way to Make Humans Immortal." *Popular Mechanics*. January 26, 2022. https://www.popularmechanics.com/technology/startups/a38867242/jeff-bezos-altos-labs/.

71 Oliver Zolman, M.D. https://www.oliverzolman.com/

72 Duckworth, Angela L., Christopher Peterson, Michael D. Matthews, and Dennis R. Kelly. "Grit: Perseverance and Passion for Long-Term Goals." *Journal of Personality and Social Psychology* 92, no. 6 (2007): 1087–1101. https://doi.org/10.1037/0022-3514.92.6.1087.

73   St-Esprit, Meg. "The Stigma of Choosing Trade School Over College." The Atlantic. Atlantic Media Company, March 7, 2019. https://www.theatlantic.com/education/archive/2019/03/choosing-trade-school-over-college/584275/.

74   Lee, Ronald. "SEC Upskilling & Reskilling: A New Retention Concept." www.army.mil, March 31, 2022. https://www.army.mil/article/255256/sec_upskilling_reskilling_a_new_retention_concept.

75   Hammer, Markus. "OPS 4.0--the Human Factor: The Need for Speed in Building Skills." McKinsey & Company, July 2022. https://www.mckinsey.com/capabilities/operations/our-insights/operations-blog/the-human-factor-in-ops-4-0-the-need-for-speed-in-building-skills.

76   Grant, Adam. *Originals: How Non-Conformists Move the World*. New York, NY: Penguin Books, an imprint of Penguin Random House LLC, 2017.

77   Janssen, Dawn, and Stephen Carradini. "Generation Z Workplace Communication Habits and Expectations." *IEEE Transactions on Professional Communication* 64, no. 2 (2021): 137–53. https://doi.org/10.1109/tpc.2021.3069288.

78   Huberman, Andrew. Controlling Your Dopamine For Motivation, Focus & Satisfaction. Other. *Huberman Lab Podcast*, 2022.

79   Steensland, Pamela. "Piper Sandler Completes 43rd Semi-Annual Generation Z Survey of 7,100 U.S. Teens. | Piper Sandler, April 2022. https://www.pipersandler.com/news/piper-sandler-completes-43rd-semi-annual-generation-z-survey-7100-us-teens.

80   Barnes, Mitchell, Lauren Bauer, and Wendy Edelberg. "Nine Facts about the Service Sector in the United States." Brookings. Brookings, September 29, 2022. https://www.brookings.edu/research/nine-facts-about-the-service-sector-in-the-united-states/.

81   Pine, Joseph, and James Gilmore. "Welcome to the Experience Economy." Harvard Business Review, August 1, 2014. https://hbr.org/1998/07/welcome-to-the-experience-economy.

82   Georgiev, Deyan. "18 Shocking OnlyFans Statistics to Show How Big It Is [2023]." Web log. *Tech Jury* (blog), March 30, 2023. https://techjury.net/blog/onlyfans-statistics/.

83   Solano, Ingrid, Nicholas R. Eaton, and K. Daniel O'Leary. "Pornography Consumption, Modality and Function in a Large Internet Sample." *The Journal of Sex Research* 57, no. 1 (2018): 92–103. https://doi.org/10.1080/00224499.2018.1532488.

84   Yoder, Vincent Cyrus, Thomas Virden , and Amin Kiran, "Internet Pornography and Loneliness: An Association?" *Sexual Addiction & Compulsivity* 12, no. 1 (2005): 19–44. https://doi.org/10.1080/10720160590933653.

85   Regnerus, Mark, David Gordon, and Joseph Price. "Documenting Pornography Use in America: A Comparative Analysis of Methodological Approaches." *The Journal of Sex Research* 53, no. 7 (2015): 873–81. https://doi.org/10.1080/0022 4499.2015.1096886.

86   "Demographics of the U.S. Military." Council on Foreign Relations. Council on Foreign Relations. Accessed April 9, 2023. https://www.cfr.org/backgrounder/demographics-us-military.

87   Lei, Lei, and Scott J. South. "Explaining the Decline in Young Adult Sexual Activity in the United States." *Journal of Marriage and Family* 83, no. 1 (2020): 280–95. https://doi.org/10.1111/jomf.12723.

88   "Thirst Trap." Urban Dictionary. Accessed April 9, 2023. https://www.urbandictionary.com/define.php?term=Thirst+Trap.

89   Roza, David. "A Marine's Anime-Style Recruitment Posters Are Going Viral." Task & Purpose, February 26, 2022. https://taskandpurpose.com/news/marine-anime-recruitment-poster/.

90   "Unplug Collaborative." Unplug Collaborative. Accessed April 9, 2023. https://www.unplugcollaborative.org/.

91   Centers for Disease Control and Prevention. 2019 Youth Risk Behavior Survey Questionnaire. Available at: www.cdc.gov/yrbs. Accessed on January 2023.

92   Fick, Nathaniel. *One Bullet Away: The Making of a Marine Officer*. London: Phoenix, 2007.

93   Philipps, Dave, and Tim Arango. "Who Signs up to Fight? Makeup of U.S. Recruits Shows Glaring Disparity." The New York *Times*. The New York Times, January 10, 2020. https://www.nytimes.com/2020/01/10/us/military-enlistment.html.

94   McQuarrie, Christopher. 2012. *Jack Reacher*. United States: Paramount Pictures.

95   Tocqueville, Alexis de. *Democracy in America*. New York: G. Dearborn & Co., 1838

96   "Shooting Incidents at K-12 Schools (Jan 1970-June 2022)." CHDS School Shooting Safety Compendium, March 2, 2023. https://www.chds.us/sssc/data-map/.

97   "Watch: Gen-z Reporter's Communication Tips Crack up Gen-X Anchors |
      CNN Business." CNN. Cable News Network, December 15, 2022. https://
      www.cnn.com/videos/media/2022/12/15/gen-z-communication-mis-
      takes-coates-camerota-cprog-ctn-vpx.cnn.

98   Sheridan, David C., Sara Grusing, Rebecca Marshall, Amber Lin, Adrienne R.
      Hughes, Robert G. Hendrickson, and B. Zane Horowitz. "Changes in Suicidal
      Ingestion among Preadolescent Children from 2000 to 2020." *JAMA Pediatrics*
      176, no. 6 (2022): 604. https://doi.org/10.1001/jamapediatrics.2022.0069.

99   Piekarz-Porter, Elizabeth, Wanting Lin, Julien Leider, Lindsey Turner, Frank
      Perna, and Jamie F Chriqui. "State Laws Matter When It Comes to School
      Provisions for Structured PE and Daily PE Participation." *Translational
      Behavioral Medicine* 11, no. 2 (2020): 597–603. https://doi.org/10.1093/tbm/
      ibaa013.

100   "George Washington's Farewell Address." George Washington's Mount Vernon,
      September 17, 1796. https://www.mountvernon.org/library/digitalhistory/
      quotes/article/however-political-parties-may-now-and-then-answer-popular-
      ends-they-are-likely-in-the-course-of-time-and-things-to-become-potent-en-
      gines-by-which-cunning-ambitious-and-unprincipled-men-will-be-enabled-to-
      subvert-the-power-of-the-people-and-to-usurp-for-th/.

101   Hall, Madison. "This One Chart Shows an Unprecedented Recent Spike
      in Age for Congress, Posing a Huge Problem for American Democracy."
      Business Insider. Accessed April 9, 2023. https://www.businessinsider.com/
      congress-oldest-history-gerontocracy-lawmakers-2022-9.

102   Fiorina, Morris P., Samuel J. Abrams, and Jeremy C. Pope. *Culture War ?: The
      Myth of a Polarized America*. Boston, MA: Longman, 2011.

103   Fiorina, Morris P. *Unstable Majorities: Polarization, Party Sorting, and Political
      Stalemate*. Stanford, CA: Hoover Institution Press, Stanford University, 2017.

104   Novemsky, Nathan, and Daniel Kahneman. "The Boundaries of Loss
      Aversion." *Journal of Marketing Research* 42, no. 2 (2005): 119–28. https://doi.
      org/10.1509/jmkr.42.2.119.62292.

105   "Fall 2022 Harvard Youth Poll." The Institute of Politics at Harvard
      University. Accessed April 9, 2023. https://iop.harvard.edu/
      youth-poll/44th-edition-fall-2022.

106   Abrams, Samuel. "Op-Ed: Gen Z's Pragmatic Politics Could Be
      a Key to Ending Polarization." Los Angeles *Times*. November 19,
      2022. https://www.latimes.com/opinion/story/2022-11-19/
      gen-z-politics-midterm-elections-voting?_amp=true.

107 Armstrong, Brian. "Coinbase is a mission focused company." Coinbase Blog, 2020. https://www.coinbase.com/blog.

108 Nindl, Bradley, and Mita Lovalekar. "USMC Gender-Integrated Recruit Training Study." *Neuromuscular Research Laboratory - University of Pittsburgh*, 2022.

109 Plante, Mauricio La. "Avoiding Confrontation, Some Republicans Live in Fear in Silicon Valley." San José Spotlight, April 9, 2020. https://sanjosespotlight.com/a-silent-majority-some-republicans-live-in-fear-in-silicon-valley/.

110 Urben, Heidi. "Like, Comment, Retweet: The State of the Military's Nonpartisan Ethic in the World of Social Media." National Defense University Press, 2017.

111 Schumm, Jeremiah, and Kathleen Chard. "Alcohol and Stress in the Military." *National Institute on Alcohol Abuse and Alcoholism* 34, no. 4 (n.d.).

112 "The Kids Are Alright: Tobacco, Alcohol and Cannabis Use Among Gen Z." Newfrontierdata.com, May 2022. https://newfrontierdata.com/cannabis-insights/the-kids-are-alright-tobacco-alcohol-and-cannabis-use-among-gen-z/#:~:text=More%20than%20two%2Dthirds%20(69,%25%20among%20ages%2065%2D74.

113 Beaton, Kelly. "Survey: Gen Z Drawn to Cannabis Products." The Food Institute, November 17, 2021. https://foodinstitute.com/focus/survey-gen-z-drawn-to-cannabis-products/.

114 Asch, Beth J., Michael L. Hansen, Rosanna Smart, David Knapp, and Daniel Schwam, An Empirical Assessment of the U.S. Army's Enlistment Waiver Policies: An Examination in Light of Emerging Societal Trends in Behavioral Health and the Legalization of Marijuana. Santa Monica, CA: RAND Corporation, 2021. https://www.rand.org/pubs/research_reports/RR4431.html

115 Hall, Wayne, and Megan Weier. "Lee Robins' Studies of Heroin Use among US Vietnam Veterans." *Addiction* 112, no. 1 (2016): 176–80. https://doi.org/10.1111/add.13584.

116 Frankl, Viktor E. *Man's Search for Meaning*. Boston, MA: Beacon Press, 2014.

117 Vultaggio, Maria, and Felix Richter. "Infographic: Gen Z Is Lonely." Statista Infographics, February 4, 2020. https://www.statista.com/chart/20713/lonlieness-america/.

118   Curtin SC, Heron M. Death rates due to suicide and homicide among persons aged 10–24: United States, 2000–2017. NCHS Data Brief, no 352. Hyattsville, MD: National Center for Health Statistics. 2019.

119   Colvin, Casey. "State of Gen Z Mental Health 2022." Healthcare Data Management Software & Services | Harmony Healthcare IT, April 12, 2023. https://www.harmonyhit.com/state-of-gen-z-mental-health/.

120   Chan, Melissa. "4 Navy Sailors Assigned to Same Facility Die by Apparent Suicide within Weeks, amid Growing Concerns of Mental Health Crisis." NBCNews.com. NBCUniversal News Group, December 1, 2022. https://www.nbcnews.com/news/us-news/4-navy-sailors-assigned-facility-die-apparent-suicide-weeks-growing-co-rcna59266.

121   Gross, Terry. "A Marine Veteran Says the Contradictions of War Can Make You Feel Insane." NPR, November 11, 2021. https://www.npr.org/2021/11/11/1054655268/former-marine-elliot-ackerman-Veterans-day.

122   Kellermann, Arthur L., John W. Saultz, Ateev Mehrotra, Spencer S. Jones, and Siddartha Dalal. "Primary Care Technicians: A Solution to the Primary Care Workforce Gap." Health Affairs 32, no. 11 (2013): 1893–98. https://doi.org/10.1377/hlthaff.2013.0481.

123   Atske, Sara. "The State of Gig Work in 2021." Pew Research Center: Internet, Science & Tech. Pew Research Center, December 8, 2021. https://www.pewresearch.org/internet/2021/12/08/the-state-of-gig-work-in-2021/.

124   Spreitzer, Gretchen, Peter Bacevice, and Lyndon Garrett. "Why People Thrive in Coworking Spaces." Harvard Business Review, November 29, 2018. https://hbr.org/2015/05/why-people-thrive-in-coworking-spaces.

125   "The Cost of Supporting Military Bases." Congressional Budget Office, November 26, 2019. https://www.cbo.gov/publication/55849.

126   Reports, Special. "Ex-Workers Say U.S. Military Landlord Forged Records to Win Bonuses." Reuters. Thomson Reuters, November 20, 2019. https://www.reuters.com/investigates/special-report/usa-military-lackland/.

127   Pinnegar, Robert. "Perspective | How Gen Z Is Shaping the Future of Apartment Living." The Washington Post. WP Company, March 31, 2022. https://www.washingtonpost.com/business/2022/03/28/how-gen-z-is-shaping-future-apartment-living/.

128   Range Commanders Council White Sands Missile Range Nm. "Commander's Guide to Community Involvement." DTIC. Accessed February 9, 2023. https://apps.dtic.mil/sti/citations/AD1158188.

129 Dolch, Norman, Helen Wise and Ronald Wade (2017) "The Impact of a Military Base on Community Volunteering: A Case Study," *Journal of Ideology*: Vol. 38: No. 1, Article 1. Available at: https://scholarcommons.sc.edu/ji/vol38/iss1/1

130 Bilandzic, Mark Vicko (2013) *The embodied hybrid space : designing social and digital interventions to facilitate connected learning in coworking spaces.* PhD by Publication, Queensland University of Technology.

131 "Demographics of the U.S. Military." Council on Foreign Relations. Accessed February 10, 2023. https://www.cfr.org/backgrounder/demographics-us-military.

132 Leukhina, Oksana, and Amy Smaldone. "Why Do Women Outnumber Men in College Enrollment?" Saint Louis Fed Eagle. Federal Reserve Bank of St. Louis, January 3, 2023. https://www.stlouisfed.org/on-the-economy/2022/mar/why-women-outnumber-men-college-enrollment#:~:text=When%20the%20fall%20college%20enrollment,seen%20in%20U.S.%20college%20enrollment.

133 Zenger, Jack, and Joseph Folkman. "Research: Women Score Higher than Men in Most Leadership Skills." *Harvard Business Review*, September 17, 2021. https://hbr.org/2019/06/research-women-score-higher-than-men-in-most-leadership-skills.

134 Goldman, Bruce. "How Men's and Women's Brains Are Different." *Stanford Medicine Magazine*, September 21, 2022. https://stanmed.stanford.edu/how-mens-and-womens-brains-are-different/.

135 Department of Defense. 2022. "The Department of Defense Annual Report on Sexual Assault in the Military." RefID: A-B4B4354.

136 Hogan, Paul F., and Rita Furst Seifert. "Marriage and the Military: Evidence That Those Who Serve Marry Earlier and Divorce Earlier." *Armed Forces & Society* 36, no. 3 (2009): 420–38. https://doi.org/10.1177/0095327x09351228.

137 Bian, Bo and Li, Jingjing and Xu, Ting and Foutz, Natasha Zhang, Individualism During Crises (July 9, 2021). Review of Economics and Statistics, Forthcoming, Available at SSRN: https://ssrn.com/abstract=3626841 or http://dx.doi.org/10.2139/ssrn.3626841

138 Jones, Jeffrey M. "LGBT Identification in U.S. Ticks up to 7.1%." Gallup.com. Gallup, June 10, 2022. https://news.gallup.com/poll/389792/lgbt-identification-ticks-up.aspx.

139 Council on Foreign Relations. "Demographics of the U.S. Military." Accessed April 9, 2023. https://www.cfr.org/backgrounder/demographics-us-military.

140 Atske, Sara. "What People around the World like – and Dislike – about American Society and Politics." Pew Research Center's Global Attitudes Project. Pew Research Center, March 22, 2022. https://www.pewresearch.org/global/2021/11/01/what-people-around-the-world-like-and-dislike-about-american-society-and-politics/.

141 Creary, Stephanie. "How to Elevate Diversity, Equity, and Inclusion Work in Your Organization." Knowledge at Wharton, July 2020. https://knowledge.wharton.upenn.edu/article/elevate-diversity-equity-inclusion-work-organization/.

142 Bump, Philip. "Analysis | the Army May Be Unprepared to Win a War against Bad-Faith Criticism." The Washington *Post*. WP Company, October 11, 2022. https://www.washingtonpost.com/politics/2022/10/11/army-tucker-carlson-recruiting/.

143 Department of Defense, Office of the Undersecretary for Policy (Strategy, Plans, and Capabilities). 2021. Department of Defense Climate Risk Analysis. Report Submitted to the National Security Council.

144 Hickman, Caroline, Elizabeth Marks, Panu Pihkala, Susan Clayton, Eric R. Lewandowski, Elouise E. Mayall, Britt Wray, Catriona Mellor, and Lise van Susteren. "Young People's Voices on Climate Anxiety, Government Betrayal and Moral Injury: A Global Phenomenon." *SSRN Electronic Journal*, 2021. https://doi.org/10.2139/ssrn.3918955.

145 Italie, Leanne. "Gen Z, Millennials Speak out on Reluctance to Become Parents." AP NEWS. Associated Press, August 30, 2022. https://apnews.com/article/covid-health-millennials-fcaa60313baf717312c6e68f12eb53ff.

146 Nadeem, Reem. "Gen Z, Millennials Stand out for Climate Change Activism, Social Media Engagement with Issue." Pew Research Center Science & Society. Pew Research Center, April 28, 2022. https://www.pewresearch.org/science/2021/05/26/gen-z-millennials-stand-out-for-climate-change-activism-social-media-engagement-with-issue/.

147 Rotondi, Flavia, and Chiara Remondini. "Cashmere Billionaire Balances Profit with Working Conditions." Bloomberg.com. Bloomberg, February 4, 2023. https://www.bloomberg.com/news/articles/2023-02-04/billionaire-cucinelli-sets-profits-cap-to-thrive-for-centuries?srnd=premium&leadSource=uverify+wall.

148 LinkedIn. "Global Green Skills Report 2022." LinkedIn, 2022. https://economicgraph.linkedin.com/research/global-green-skills-report.

149 Liebermann, Oren, Haley Britzky, Michael Conte, and Nectar Gan. "Pentagon Tracking Suspected Chinese Spy Balloon over the US | CNN Politics." CNN. Cable News Network, February 3, 2023. https://www.cnn.com/2023/02/02/politics/us-tracking-china-spy-balloon/index.html.

150 Brose, Christian. The kill chain: Defending America in the future of high-tech warfare. New York, NY: Hachette Books, Hachette Book Group, 2020.

151 Wong, Brian. "The Complex Nationalism of China's Gen-z." – The Diplomat. for The Diplomat, June 23, 2022. https://thediplomat.com/2022/06/the-complex-nationalism-of-chinas-gen-z/.

152 Fang, Lee. "Twitter Aided the Pentagon in Its Covert Online Propaganda Campaign." The Intercept. The Intercept, December 20, 2022. https://theintercept.com/2022/12/20/twitter-dod-us-military-accounts/.

153 Haass, Richard. The Bill of Obligations: The Ten Habits of Good Citizens. New York: Penguin Press, 2023.

154 Mineo, Liz. "Over Nearly 80 Years, Harvard Study Has Been Showing How to Live a Healthy and Happy Life." Harvard Gazette, April 5, 2023. https://news.harvard.edu/gazette/story/2017/04/over-nearly-80-years-harvard-study-has-been-showing-how-to-live-a-healthy-and-happy-life/.

155 Zoldra, Paul. "Award-Winning Journalist Perfectly Captures the Reason Soldiers Often Miss Combat." Business Insider. Accessed April 18, 2023. https://www.businessinsider.com/sebastian-junger-veterans-miss-war-2014-6?amp.

156 Dalio, Ray. Principles. New York: Simon and Schuster, 2017.

Made in United States
Troutdale, OR
08/30/2023

12497844R00147